Dreaming of a Mail-Order Husband

⟨ Russian-American Internet Romance ⟩

Ericka Johnson

Duke University Press   Durham and London   2007

© 2007 Duke University Press
All rights reserved
Printed in the United States of America on acid-free paper ∞
Designed by Heather Hensley
Typeset in Bembo by Keystone Typesetting, Inc.
Library of Congress Cataloging-in-Publication data appear on
the last printed page of this book.

The author has donated royalties to the Kvinna till
Kvinna Foundation, which supports women's organizations in
conflict regions, strengthening women's physical and
psychological health and increasing their confidence and ability
to participate in building democratic societies.

To the women
*who have shared their
stories with me.*

Contents

Acknowledgments

*D*uring the writing of this work, I received input and support from several different intellectual communities. The project began as research in development studies at the Queen Elizabeth House and Somerville College, Oxford University, England. Its early form and gestation owes much to the suggestions and guidance I received from David Mills and Cathie Lloyd. I was able to continue working on it thanks to the intellectual freedom and infrastructural space I have found at the Department of Technology and Social Change, Linköping University, Sweden. There, above all, I have been able to benefit from a wonderful community of scholars interested in technology and gender, including Boel Berner, Nina Lykke, Ulf Mellström, Minna Salminen-Karlsson, Petra Jonvallen, and Francis Lee. Final work on the manuscript was done at the Institute for Advanced Studies on Science, Technology and Society in Graz, Austria, where I found the quiet calm that manuscript preparation requires combined with friendly exchange and encouragement from fellow scholars. Thank you to Michelle McGowan, Bettina Bock von Wülfingen, Kyra Landzelius, Günter Getzinger, and Harald Rohracher. The helpful comments from three anonymous reviewers and my editors, Miriam Angress and Pam Morrison, have shaped this book for the better. Alex Klimoff helped me with Russian language questions, and, most important, inspired me to study in Russia in the first place. And if it were not for the personal encouragement, support, and help from Anders, Russ, and Winnie, this book would never have been written. Thank you.

Introduction

*W*hen Russian mail-order brides appear in American news reports and TV documentaries,[1] they are usually connected to stories of abuse, domestic violence, and human trafficking. Often these brides are described as victims, trapped in horrible marriages with lonely, imbalanced men. Sometimes they are portrayed as gold diggers looking for economic stability and a green card. Occasionally they are shown as women married to American husbands who are helping them adjust to life in the United States. Rarely, however, are they allowed an active role in these portrayals. The women are contacted, courted, married, imported, abused, or cared for by men. They are the direct object of American attention, for better or worse. Seldom are they allowed to be the subject of their own activities.

This book tries to offer an alternative. It is about six women from the former Soviet Union, who have met men through listings on the Internet. It is a study about how and why the women have placed themselves on Internet matchmaking sites. Rather than writing about foreign romances, trafficking, or mail-order brides in general, I use this book to let these women themselves speak. This is a highly problematic assertion: I, as the author, am still interpreting what they say, in some cases translating their words, and always co-opting their voices. But I am also trying as best I can to present their perspectives and reflections on why and how they have chosen to meet foreign men through the Internet. To try to give the reader a feeling for the details of the world these women inhabit, I have included anecdotes from when I studied in Russia during the mid-1990s. Including my own experiences in the text this way can give this book a personal memoir style, but I hope that the reader will see these anecdotes as a way of describing what the Russian transitional economy looks like on the ground and in daily life. I also hope they can show how the women's descriptions and explanations of their activities are influenced by their own personal life experiences and that I, as an outsider, had a special relationship to their context. While I cannot hope to convey or even construct any detailed understanding of these individuals' personal backgrounds from an interview or a few exchanged correspondences, I can try to give the reader a feeling for how I, as an American, experienced life in Russia and perhaps thereby also create a contextual background against which the reader can place the interviews and the other academic research I cite.

I work in the field of gender and technology, and this book stems from a study originally designed to examine the spread of IT to and within the former Soviet Union. It is based on interviews with Russian women both there and in the United States, women who were writing to American men or who had moved to America to live with a man they had met "online." When I began the project in the late 1990s I did so by purchasing the addresses of women listed with a Russian mail-order bride website and writing them a letter in which I introduced myself and the study. I sent that letter to eighty-eight women, asking them if they would be willing to participate. A few of those letters were returned unopened, and some probably got lost in the mail, but from the ones that made it to their destination, nineteen women wrote back to me. Many of these women said they would be willing to meet me in person, and when I traveled to the former Soviet Union a few months later, I interviewed fourteen women, two of whom were also working as local matchmaking agents.[2] A few years after the initial project, I took up the research again and interviewed individuals in the United States who were involved in Russian-American relationships, seven in total, this time both men and women.

Most of the interviews I conducted in the former Soviet Union were done in Russian, though a few of the women I spoke with saw our meeting as an opportunity to practice their English, and in those cases we spoke in English. The interviews I have recreated here are from notes taken during and after those interviews. Names and other identifying details have been changed throughout the text. In a couple of more sensitive cases, to protect the identities of the women I interviewed, I have created their personae based on composites of several different interviews. The interviews with women in the United States were conducted in English, but when writing them up for the book, I fixed grammatical structures in the interview transcripts, mostly adding articles and correcting verb tenses. These are aspects of spoken English that Russians sometimes have difficulties with, and I decided to change them for two reasons: first, it makes the text easier for a native English speaker to read, and my aim is to express the content of what the women are saying, not their specific way of speaking; and also because the English in the translated interviews would have otherwise appeared much "better" than the language in the interviews conducted in English, unjustly creating an apparent difference between the women in their ability to articulate feelings and ideas. So, reader beware: the interviews that follow have been reconstructed, some have been translated, and others have been "touched up." But the meaning of what the women said comes through.

The group of people I have spoken with is self-selected, and their self-selection can influence my results. This raises questions about the women I met. Why did these women, and not others, reply to my letter? Are they more or less satisfied with their matchmaking experiences than others? Are they more positive or negative about the options available to them than other Russian women? Are they more reflective about their activities than many of the others whose photographs are listed on the Internet? I will never know the answers to these questions, and yes, my study is skewed because of the character of the empirical material.[3] But that is part of doing a study like this. All samples are necessarily skewed. Likewise, my analysis of the material creates another layer of interpretation. This is an unavoidable element of social science research. I cannot claim that this study tells a whole and unadulterated truth about Russian women and foreign men. I can only hope that this book will stimulate a more nuanced discussion about their relationships. I also hope it will prompt recognition that the terms "Russian woman" and "Russian mail-order bride" describe an extremely varied group of individuals.

In writing this book, I have chosen to detail the experiences of the six women presented here because they each bring out aspects of their search that are different from the others, yet at the same time their stories of what they did, whom they met through the letters, and how they reflect on their contact with Western men resonate with the comments I heard from others during this research. Their experiences are in some way typical, yet they are each unique. That is one of the points I want to make with this book: "Russian mail-order bride" is a much more heterogeneous category than tends to be presented and understood by the matchmaking industry, in the media, and in activist debates against the phenomenon. As telling as the six narratives presented here are, however, it is true that there are many more stories to write. Thousands, perhaps tens of thousands of Russian women are writing to Western men and each of them has her own reasons for doing so. In addition, the correspondence generated in these courtships touches and involves other people the women know. Some of these contacts appear tangentially in the book. Predictably, parts of this book reflect on the men in America, and in other countries, with whom the women meet and correspond. But the cast of characters does not end there. Their stories also involve children, usually from first marriages to Russian men, who are co-participants in the relationships that develop. And importantly, it turned out that these stories often involve the older generation, too. In fact, I met mothers of both Russian women and American men who played significant parts in trying to develop the international marriages that are detailed. These "supporting characters" in the narratives highlight the point that the term "Russian mail-order bride" can really be conceived of as a trope which hides a myriad of relationships and actors.

Why these six and not others? The simple reason is that I was most moved by these six, but their experiences say much about the difficulties of life for women in the post-Soviet society. Although, in the early 1990s, the Soviet Union dissolved and the republics it had comprised became independent states, many of these states are still loosely federated (as the term Commonwealth of Independent States indicates); this commonwealth is contentious in a number of the republics, which has contributed to political instability, ethnic conflicts, and minority status for the Russians living in them. The switch from communism (at least in name), with a strictly planned economy and a tightly woven social welfare net, to (robber baron) capitalism has created extreme hardship for some of the population and allowed others to accrue fantastic wealth. The transitional period has also involved general economic instability, job losses, sporadic bouts of hyper-inflation, and a currency that is not always reliable. It is not clear whether, or how, matters will improve. Therefore, much of what the women say should be understood against the context of their lives in the postcommunist landscape. Their decisions to write to men abroad and the opinions they form from these correspondences are flavored by structural influences on their daily lives.

My original research project was an analysis of the spread of technology in the former Soviet Union and whether men and women had different levels of access to computers and the Internet. These issues are important, but I realized that there was much more involved in what the women are doing than could be addressed with this limited focus. I felt that there were more details about the practices of Russian women writing to foreign men that should be examined. How did they find out about these matchmaking sites? Why were they interested in foreign men? What kind of responses did their listings generate? How many found "love and happiness"? These were questions I wanted to answer as well. When I started to write this book, I tried to contextualize the material I gathered in the interviews, about IT usage and much else, against academic research on women, work, family life, and feminism across the former Soviet Union. To answer many of the questions my material raised, I took an interdisciplinary approach, relying on work from fields as diverse as sociology, anthropology, economics, international relations, Slavic studies, even literary studies. I also wanted to touch on the feminist debates about whether mail-order brides are trafficked women or if they are free agents. But this proved to be very difficult. The material I gathered tended to problematize the discursive framework of these debates more than it suggested answers. The perspective my informants shared with me served to dislodge my original understandings of mail-order marriage and the impact of IT on the international political economy of desire more than it gave me simple answers.

Yet, as vital as other research is to explain why and how the women are meeting foreign men, analysis of the technology they use is still relevant.

When I conducted the interviews, in the late 1990s, the women I met had extremely limited access to the Internet. What existed was very expensive, beyond the means of most of them. Five years later, when I interviewed Russian brides in the United States, it was obvious that access to the Internet had changed significantly. Many of the women I spoke with in America were in close contact with their families back home through the Internet, and several of them had even been in regular contact by e-mail with their husbands before they moved to the United States. This is influencing the transnational aspects of the relationships being developed and maintained. However, the option of regular and affordable access is still not a reality for all women in the former Soviet Union. In the development of Russian-American romances, e-mail, chat, and affordable long distance telephone calls are complementing the letters traditionally associated with mail-order brides, but letters are still a common way of developing initial contact between partners.

These are the academic details behind the work presented here and the style in which it is written. But there was another motivating factor behind my decision to write this book. After I had reported my initial results on Internet access patterns, I found I could not stop thinking about what the women I had met had said and done, and wondering how they were progressing in their search for a husband. The material would not let go of me, and I felt there was much more to be said about and, importantly, *by* the Russian mail-order brides I had met. So I sat down to write, again. This book is an attempt to finally let them speak about their actions and their dreams. My intention is to highlight the thoughts and understandings of Russian mail-order brides and address the fact that they have generally been objectified, silenced, and discussed in the media and on websites but rarely given the opportunity to speak for themselves.

A Catalogue of Women

*O*ne afternoon, early in my stay as an exchange student in Russia, I had been invited back to a new friend's apartment for dinner. We chatted in the sitting room, looking at pictures of her childhood and talking about her hopes to land a job as a singer, while her mother made dinner in the kitchen. The smells that started wafting out to where we sat were making my stomach rumble, and when we were finally called in to eat, I was both hungry and excited to be treated to a home-cooked Russian meal. The food was already dished up when we sat down at the little table, and Natasha's mother smiled warmly as she encouraged us to eat. I said "thank you," picked up my spoon, and looked into my bowl only to realize that the "chicken" in my chicken soup consisted of one boiled claw standing straight up out of the broth. Natasha and her mother both had bowls of broth with little pieces of onion floating in them, but I, as the guest, had been given the claw to chew on. It was the first time I had been invited home with Natasha; I knew they didn't have very much money, and I understood that I was being treated as the guest of honor. So, I delicately picked up the claw, smiled my appreciation at both of them, and ate what I could of it.

Natasha was one of the first women I met in Russia, and she had impressed me with her self-confidence, her talent, and her determination. Because of this, I had been more than a little surprised when, after we had finished our soup and were drinking tea and eating teaspoons of jam, she confided that she was listed with a matchmaking agency offering Russian women to American men. She seemed so independent and ambitious that I found it difficult to reconcile her personality with the desire to be an imported housewife. But she was serious about her chances of finding a husband that way.

This was in the mid-1990s, before the Internet had really taken off, and Natasha's picture had been printed up in a black-and-white catalogue and mailed out to interested men. Because of that one picture, she had received letters from about fifteen men, and when I asked her about them she eagerly put her teacup down to dig the letters out of her drawer and show them to me. We spent the next hour poring over photos and words from men who were interested in Natasha, and she asked for my help pinpointing where they lived on the map of North America in her mother's atlas. As she opened up to me, it became clear that Natasha was no longer attractive to local men, having reached the ripe old age of twenty-three. This surprised me at first, but as the year wore on, I gradually realized it was true. Women in Russia, at least in the provincial town where I was studying, were expected to have been married by her age. There were not that many men who would want to marry a *devushka* as old as Natasha. She was constantly being approached by married men, but because she wanted more than a romantic affair, she thought an American husband might be a better solution.

I had tried to ask her why she felt it was so important to get married, especially since she was busy building her career, but I could tell she thought it was odd I would even formulate a question like that. To her, it was essential she find a husband, and she was very serious about the possibilities her American letters contained. I was not overly impressed with the men who were writing to her, and several of the letters were so poorly put together that even Natasha could see that she wrote English better than those men did, but she was nonetheless willing to give most of them a chance and had started correspondence with several of them. During the rest of the evening I helped her formulate a couple of letters, translated some of the colloquialisms the men had used, and then just listened as she told me her daydreams about life as a wife in the United States.

That was more than ten years ago, but I was reminded of Natasha a few years later when I was working on a research project about the spread of information technology in the former Soviet Union. I was trying to gather some preliminary data about Internet usage in a certain city, and I had typed the city's name into an Internet search engine, hoping to find listings of service providers, cyber cafes, and possibly even IT courses at the local university. But the search results gave me none of those things. Instead I found a short page of CIA facts about the region, a personal home page by someone who had recently visited the place, and page after page of biographical details from Russian women who were trying to find husbands in the West. Instead of the names and prices of local e-mail service providers, I found "Ludmila, 24, I want a kind, serious, honest, caring, well-off man who loves children"; "Irina, 30, I am kind, good-mixer, cheerful, romantic, honest, humorous, and loyal. I can only speak a little English"; and "Svetlana, 20, cheerful, soft, faithful, humorous, loving woman. I like music and sports. I especially like knitting and sewing. I also like pets."

For a brief moment, sitting there at my computer, I smiled wryly at the irony that the city's cyberspace identity was made up of women who were trying to leave it. My smile disappeared quickly, though, as I started surfing through the women's pages and the other parts of the "International Matchmaking" site to which they belonged. I soon started feeling queasy. The section of the site I had surfed into was just one of many for the various regions of the former Soviet Union and Eastern Europe, and there were thousands of pages listing women like Ludmila, Irina, and Svetlana. And as I surfed around a little more, I realized that the company I had found was a small part of a large industry listing available women around the world. I knew that Russian mail-order brides had become more common in recent years, but until I came across those pages, I had no idea that there were so very *many* of them on the Internet.[1] Or that the women were literally being presented as potential wives to be "purchased" from the companies which were marketing them.

But aside from my shock over the sheer quantity of women on the sites, my repulsion was stirred by the obvious objectification and commodification that the pages contained. I was surfing through a veritable catalogue of goods. And I mean literally. One typical site let me search its databases of women in different ways. I could view listings of the women whose pictures had just arrived that week or of all the women from a certain city or region; I could run a query against the database and find the women who met my demands for specified physical and social characteristics—all women under twenty-five with blonde hair and no children, for example. And regardless of how I refined my search, I was presented with page after page of small thumbnail images of women who were waiting to write to me. Or, more precisely, who were waiting to write to a future husband in North America, Europe, Australia, or New Zealand. Next to each image was the woman's first name, her age, height, and weight, and when I clicked on one of these headshots, the woman's individual page appeared with a larger photo and her personal details. I could see a full body shot, read her biographical description, and, if I was still interested, I could click on the button which let me "add number 90541 to my shopping cart."

The "shopping cart" button was only one indication that the women were being presented as objects for sale. In "satisfied customer" testimonials sprinkled throughout the site and on separate pages dedicated to the virtues of Russian brides, this consumption rhetoric was rationalized by saying that the women, as such, were not for sale, it was only their addresses that were being sold. And to be fair, this was literally true. But the overwhelming impression given by the site was just the opposite. The way the women's identities were presented for potential husbands also helped the process. Each woman's page was dominated by a large picture of her, taking up the entire left side of my screen. In some cases it was a snapshot, an amateur photo of the woman peeking out between two birch trees, or on a lake shore, posing in a swim suit. But most of the photos looked like studio portraits, showing women who were professionally made-up and standing in obviously choreographed poses like shop window mannequins.

Below each woman's main photograph was a link that took me to another page of three or four additional images. Here the women were shown in different outfits, usually a swimsuit, a revealing dress, and another more matronly outfit, plus a close-up of the woman's face. The impression these images gave, along with the larger, first-page picture, was of women who were consciously and successfully balancing on the tenuous line between madonna and whore. I remember, for example, one image of a woman in a long pink floral dress with a button-front, puffy sleeves, and a white lace collar, a dress that would be appropriate at a Sunday service in any conservative church in the American Midwest. But in this picture, the dress happened to be unbuttoned from the hem to the upper thigh, with two shapely calves seductively peeking out of the slit, displaying legs and stiletto heels that would be more appropriate for Saturday night.

However, despite the obvious *double entente* in the photos, the personal descriptions of the women tended to tip their virtual identities toward ideals of domesticity and motherhood. Next to the photograph on each woman's page was a written summary of her identity, or at least those characteristics which were deemed important in helping the men judge her relative market value: physical details like age, weight, height, hair and eye color, and measurements in inches and centimeters, social details like university degrees and job descriptions, and whether the woman smoked, had children, and went to church.

Beneath all this, at the bottom of the page, were personal descriptions of the women: fifteen to twenty words that the women used to describe themselves and their interests, along with fifteen to twenty words explaining what kind of man they were hoping to find. There were recurring themes in these descriptions—ideas about family life, domesticity, and loyalty, both given and received. A typical self-description could read: "I am intelligent, kind, faithful, tender, loving, caring, romantic, cheerful and I love children. I have a son age 10." Many of the women listed their hobbies, the type of literature they liked, or their passion for classical music. And suspiciously many of the women mentioned a love of cooking, knitting, and aerobics, as if there was a rumor circulating that those hobbies garnered a positive response from the audience they were addressing.

The descriptions of what type of men they wished to meet were also fairly homogenous, though what they were describing seemed to be generally desirable characteristics for any person to have, as a husband or otherwise: "I would like to meet an honest, sociable, strong and caring man (aged 25–40) with whom I can enjoy life"; or "I wish to meet an honest man, courageous, faithful, sincere, and kind. Up to age 43." An age limit appeared quite frequently in these descriptions, and I wondered if the women were aware it was likely they would be approached by even older men and were trying to dissuade letters from unwelcome candidates.

It was in these descriptions that I found the glimmer of a counterbalance to the commodification that was so glaring in the rest of the site. Everywhere else the women were voiceless images to be clicked on, evaluated, and placed in shopping carts. Yet in the personal descriptions and lists of characteristics they wanted to find in a man, the women seemed to be whispering about their dreams and hopes, flagging their uniqueness as individuals. But that whisper was hard to hear through the sheer number of clickable, consumable images smiling loudly on the screen.

Apart from being disturbed by the sites I had surfed, though, I did not really know what to make of the phenomenon my search had presented. I had a faint suspicion that I was seeing the public face of a shadow industry for trafficking women. What I had read on the subject supported this, since mail-order brides are often listed along with other forms of human trafficking.[2] I also had the feeling I was probably viewing something that involved at least elements of the infamous Russian mafia, with their leather coats, "imported" Mercedes (stolen in Western Europe), and violent business tactics. And, not least of all, after reading the plethora of home pages lauding the benefits of "having" a Russian bride, there was little doubt I had come across a forum for an awful lot of not-so-very-enlightened, or not even socially competent, Western men who were keen on importing these women. But there was something else that made these sites unique. While using computers to find a partner is becoming more popular, as a concept it is not really that new. As early as the 1960s computers were being used to match individuals with potential mates,[3] and today's Internet dating services are not limited to mail-order bride sites and international relationships. The Internet is also a way of meeting potential partners locally, not just across international borders. The United States leads the ranks in terms of sheer numbers of dating sites and users,[4] and as in the online Russian mail-order bride databases, the criteria for finding a partner on the North American dating sites tend to be centered around physical characteristics like age, height, weight, and some social signifiers such as career choices and personal likes and dislikes. Just as I later found out that Russian women prefer Internet sites to paper catalogues, North American users also find the flexibility and available space for their personal descriptions on the Internet preferable to the limited word-counts newspapers and magazines allow.[5] And despite the limited space given, even in paper media, people find ways to personalize their information and creatively present their human sides.[6] However, one way in which the mail-order bride sites differ significantly from other dating services is that they give the impression that there are literally thousands of beautiful, smiling women who are breathlessly waiting to meet the single man who is surfing alone at his computer, a knight in shining armor who can sweep his bride away to a future of love and economic stability. This is not a situation most men encounter on a regular basis otherwise.[7]

It was then, as I was clicking through those pages, that I remembered what had happened to Natasha a few months after she had shown me her letters. I had not seen her for most of the fall semester because she had taken a singing job on a cruise ship and was gone for long stretches of time. When we finally met up again, early in the winter, it was a different Natasha I spoke with, one who was not at all as interested in the possibility of finding a man in America. After a couple of cups of tea the reason came out. She told me that one of the men I had helped her write to had flown to Russia. He had asked her to come to Moscow to meet him, which was an expensive, overnight train trip, but she was interested in him and happy he had flown to Russia at all, so she had traveled there willingly.

What the man had not told her, however, was that he had also asked three other women to do the same thing. When she arrived in Moscow, Natasha realized that she was not the only candidate vying for his affections. She said she felt humiliated and misled, but she really wanted to be the one he chose, so she tried not to show her disappointment. She had spent the week going to museums with him, sharing romantic dinners, and then following them up with romantic nights, all the time aware that he was doing the same thing with other women on the evenings they were not together.

Even though she had done her best to be desirable, worn her most seductive clothing, and spent hours ensuring that her hair and make-up were perfect, he chose one of the other women. Natasha was tall, and she said she had been surprised by how short the man was. The height difference had not really mattered to her, but she thought it could have been a problem for him, since he had commented on it several times when they were walking together in public. Whether it was because of her height or for some other reason, Natasha was not the one he chose. She said the whole experience was really humiliating, and had turned her off American men, or at least ones that she met from letters. I told her she was probably making the right decision, and she laughed somewhat bitterly at the thought of a man who would spend a thousand dollars flying to Russia only to discover the woman he was interested in was too tall. "I'm not going to bother answering any more men," she said.

Yet, a few weeks later, she asked me for help translating another letter. I kept my comments to myself and helped her willingly, but I was still confused about what was driving her. What I could not understand was her desire for a self-sufficient career, her drive and strength as an individual, and her wish to be a wife to the sort of man she was getting letters from. So when, several years later, I was confronted with the web pages of many, many women doing just what Natasha had done, I immediately wondered about what was driving them, as well. I therefore shifted the focus of my research slightly and designed a study that examined how the women came in contact with the mail-order bride agencies, before they had moved (or been moved) abroad, and why they were trying to find a husband that way.

The first step of my study was to get in touch with the women. The most straightforward way to do this was to purchase their addresses on the Web, just like a potential suitor would do. I chose a company, figured out how their online ordering system worked, and bought a "gold membership." With my credit card and my membership number written on a small piece of paper, I was able to order the addresses of as many women as I wanted, which I proceeded to do. I went out to the women's pages on the site and began adding 90798, 69802, 34863, and so on to my "shopping cart."

I chose to limit the study by selecting a smaller city and contacting all of the women living there who were listed with the company. It was an unsettling feeling to work my way through their pages, looking at each woman's picture and her details, and then clicking on the "order" button to buy her address. I felt as if I were exploiting the women myself, by paying the company that had put them in a virtual catalogue. I had read the reassurances from the company's site that I was only buying addresses, and that it was up to me to develop a relationship with the women, but it still felt as if I were buying *them*.

Within twenty-four hours my "order" was filled and I received an e-mail with the full names and post addresses (in both the Latin and Cyrillic alphabets) of eighty-eight different women. I then sat down and composed a letter to each of the women, in which I introduced myself as a female academic interested in their use of Internet-based international matchmaking agencies. I asked the women how they had originally gotten in touch with the agency, and what sort of application process they had gone through. I inquired about the number and quality of responses they had received and how they communicated with the men. I also asked them why they had decided to start this correspondence in the first place, and if their experiences had changed their impressions about Western men and international relationships.

About a quarter of the women replied. And what stories their letters contained. One of the women was convinced that I was actually a man, trying to trick her into revealing her real feelings, but all the other women took my questions at face value and replied in emotionally charged, painfully honest, and thoughtful words about their experiences. And across the board their responses echoed the answer I received from Larissa, who wrote, "Like most women, I want to have a family, a loving husband, believe in tomorrow and know that my fate depends on me, and not on the political and economical situation of my country." The women explained the logic of their searchers and opened their souls to me.

I had written the letters in English, since I assumed that most of the men would also write in English, and I was curious about what methods the women used to translate the letters. But I also wrote a postscript in Russian, explaining that they were perfectly welcome to write back in Russian if that was easier. As I suspected would be the case, most of the women replied in Russian, saying they usually used the help of others (friends, relatives, or professional translators) to correspond with the men in English. A couple of the women confided that they had tried to write to men in Russian, but that none of the men had bothered to find a translator for their letters. Instead, their letters had been returned unread, the men insisting that the women rewrite in English.

I also asked if they would be willing to be interviewed in person and discuss their experiences with me, and quite a few of them said they would. So after a little bureaucratic hassle getting a visa and finding a plane ticket to the little city, I left for the former Soviet Union. The women I had been in touch with met me in city parks, at cafes, and in their homes, and they also introduced me to others they knew who were writing to men through other companies and therefore had not received my letter. The youngest of the women I met had just turned nineteen, and a couple of them were well over forty, but most were somewhere in their late twenties. None of the women were particularly well off, but except for one, they were all employed or studying. And across the board they described what they were doing as trying to find their future happiness, which for them involved a husband and a family.

Many of the women I met had listed themselves on the Internet with the help of local agents, and one of the women I had written to was moonlighting as an agent herself. Another of my contacts put me in touch with a different agent while I was in town. Both of these were Russian women who had collected the addresses and application forms from different matchmaking companies and then charged other women a fee for help in completing the form and sending off their information.[8] These agents were well informed about the type of men available and the best way to attract their attention, and their knowledge about the market's desires helped explain why there was a certain predictability in the "personal descriptions" on the Web.

But information about what the men were interested in was not a professional secret. There seemed to be a general consensus among all the women I met that Western men want thin, attractive women who are more interested in being a wife and mother than in having a career. At first it surprised me that there was such widespread agreement between the women over what the men were looking for, but when the women showed me letters they had already received, I had to admit that they seemed to have understood correctly. This knowledge was something they shared with each other when starting the process and when comparing notes on the letters they had received, and it turned out that no one I met was looking for a husband on her own. Those who were not working with one of the agents had often decided to send off their application along with a friend or two, or because they knew someone else who was already writing to men. Knowledge about the market of men they were accessing spread like wildfire through these subcommunities.[9]

The interviews had shown me the detailed practices the women employed in order to make their applications and listings successful and to attract letters from the "right" type of men. When I finished conducting them, I headed back to my university and wrote up the study's results. I thought about how the women had all been adamant about the importance of listing themselves on Internet sites instead of with the more traditional paper catalogues. And I tried to contextualize this conscious decision to use the Internet within the "unconnected" reality of the women's daily practice. At the time I had been there, of all the women I met, only one had ever surfed the Net, only the two agents had e-mail addresses, and most of the women had never even sat in front of a computer, much less a computer with a modem. In fact, several of the women did not even have telephones. Yet at some level they were all consciously and successfully using the Internet.[10]

Analyzing this within the theoretical framework of technology transfer, I drew conclusions about the importance of recognizing alternative IT usage patterns. But it felt as if the results I had written were missing something. I felt that I had left out an important part of the study: the women themselves. I could not get them out of my head, especially their feelings and descriptions about what they were doing. I could not forget the experiences with Western men they had told me about and their desire to share that knowledge with others. I felt that the important aspects of their activities—their resourcefulness, their control over whom to write to and what to reveal about themselves while still in their own country, and above all their desire to find a partner—were not coming through, either in the report from my study or in the media reports I had seen elsewhere about mail-order brides. And I wondered what happened to the women once they moved abroad to be with their mail-order husbands. I also felt that I was a little bit closer to understanding Natasha and her determination to find an American husband. But none of this had much to do with IT usage. So in the end I decided to continue the research, interviewing Russian brides in America and writing another version of this study, not focusing on how the women do or do not use the Internet, or how they exploit or are exploited by the opportunities the technology offers them and others. Instead I have written about the women and their understandings of what this international correspondence means to them.

The interviews I conducted, both in the former Soviet Union and the United States, made it clear that the women who are trying to find mail-order husbands cannot be placed in a single category, even though they often are, both by the men interested in writing to the women and by academics and activists discussing the mail-order bride phenomenon. When analyzing my material, I noticed that there were similarities between what the Russian women shared with me and what other research has discovered about international marriages between women in Asia or Latin America and American men: their desire to be a wife and mother, their responses to a perceived positionality in their home countries which prevents them from attaining those goals, and their ideas about how life will be in the United States when they move there and begin to integrate into their new communities, both at home and at work. Like Russian women, Asian and Latin American women are also perceived and portrayed as better mothers and wives, more traditional and loyal, and less competitive and career-oriented by potential husbands and the industry. Yet there are also some differences. The whiteness of Russian women differentiates them (or at least the discourse about them) from the more established markets of Asian and Latin American mail-order brides. There is not as much discussion about the importance of new, strong genetic material found in advertisements about why a Russian woman is the perfect bride, as one finds, for example, in discussion groups about brides from Latin America.[11] Instead, on the websites about Russian brides, the women are usually described in terms of the perfect wife: happy to marry an older, less attractive man, even though they are young and beautiful themselves; content to take care of the family and home; uninterested in a career; and willing to let the man take his proper position as head of the household.

This one-sided stereotype is strengthened by the fact that the women's biographies are taken from simplistic application forms that dictate the types of questions the women can answer, which topics they can address, and how much space they are given to do so in.

The mirror image of this docile mail-order bride is the economically desperate woman who will do anything to migrate to the West. Her circumstances either make her an easy victim of unscrupulous men or create a gold digger who uses her beauty and charms on an unsuspecting husband.

The women I met, however, belie both of these stereotypes. The former Soviet Union has become a large and diverse collection of republics, provinces, nationalities, and ethnic groups, and this variation is reflected in the population of women searching for husbands abroad. The material realities of daily life, everything from access to fresh vegetables, a stable supply of hot water, or electricity, can vary widely between the life of a Muscovite and that of a woman living in the provinces. City life in general, even in the provinces, is years ahead of the life in the villages,[12] where many homes still use wood stoves for heating, cooking, and warming water. And even within a single town, the extreme class differences which have emerged during the economic reforms of the last fifteen years make using the term "Russian woman" problematic. Each of the women I met was placed differently in the intersections of class, education, gender, ethnicity, and regional identity. They came from widely varying backgrounds, social and economic situations, and educational levels. Some were still in school, some were successfully employed, and others were treading water in the new economic order. Some were young, pliable, and traditionally feminine, as the website rhetoric claimed Russian women were. Others were older, established women with well-developed identities and tough survival skills. Lifestyles, personal backgrounds, and future goals varied widely among these women. To imagine Russian mail-order brides only as economically desperate, delicate young things is to overlook the diversity that exists among them.

To reflect this, in the pages that follow, six women are given the space to present themselves that their online bios denied them. Each woman had different expectations going into her mail-order husband project and each has had different experiences with the correspondence it generated. When I met Olga, she was a young student still living at home, but her mother was worried about what her future held and the lack of opportunities for her in the job market. It was Olga's mother who had encouraged her to secure a future abroad by finding a husband. Vera, who was thirty-two at the time we met, was divorced, living with her mother and her son, and running her own "international matchmaking agency" out of the travel agency where she worked. She was convinced that her services provided women with the chance to find happiness, so much so that she had also written to men abroad and had traveled to the United States to "test drive" a relationship. It had not worked out, but she was still adamant that the right man was out there waiting for her.

Valentina, in her late thirties, was trying to find a man with whom she could share her interests and experiences. She was well educated and had been married once, long ago, but divorced after only a couple of years. She had been taking care of herself for the last fifteen years. Valentina was independent, but she missed the companionship a husband could provide and hoped to find that through the mail. When I met Tanya, who was twenty-one, beautiful, and also writing to a number of men, I was surprised to discover that she was already married. She assured me bitterly that her marriage was over, and it was just the formal divorce that she was still waiting for. She told me she was going to the States in a couple of weeks to stay with a friend and maybe meet a man she had been writing to. However, her sister, who had introduced us, gave me a different story. She said Tanya had come in contact with a Russian company which promised her a visa to the United States, and she had just sold her apartment to raise money for the fee they demanded. I tried to warn Tanya about the trafficking that occurred with women her age, but she assured me she was going to work as a waitress, that she was very careful, and that she knew what she was doing. And she was determined to go.

Marina had corresponded with a man in the United States, and their relationship had developed beyond the letters and e-mails into marriage. Now they were living in a small American town and dealing with the culture shock and adjustments that moving to another country entails. And like Olga, Marina also got help finding her husband from an older generation. Anastasia and John, in the final interview, are a Russian-American couple who are making their life together, going through the daily trials and tribulations that any marriage brings with it and also tackling the cultural differences between them. Anastasia's comment at the end of our discussion resonated poignantly with what other women had shared with me. She said that if she could give other women one piece of advice, it would be, "Don't try to find a new place to live in, try to find a person."

I am sure the other women I spoke with would agree with her. But because these women were all different, each had something unique to say to other women who are looking for husbands in the mail. And, importantly for those who may be "successful" and move abroad to be with a husband, each of them has something to say to those in the West whom they will eventually meet. What comes through in their stories is that because the mail-order bride phenomenon is so very widespread, there is not *one* type of Russian bride. But that said, as different as the women are, they do have one thing in common: the longing for a better future and the belief that having a husband and a family is an important component of that future. Or, as one of the women wrote to me at the end of her letter,

> I think that, like all women, I deserve happiness. I want to have more children, give my son a good education, and believe in tomorrow. It is possible that I am capable of giving happiness to a man, and in the end it isn't important what nationality he is; English, French, American or Italian. What is important is that we are soul mates and have the same goal: the creation of friendship and a harmonious family. I know that I will be a good wife, and you, as a woman, I think you can understand my desire to find a friend and a husband.

Ironically, it is the desire for a husband and family that can make a woman take the extreme step of leaving her country, her friends, and the family she already has to find her future with a foreign man. And it is that desire to find a friend and a husband abroad that I will let the women in this book explain.

{ 2 }

Olga: Feminism or Femininity

*O*lga suggested we meet for the interview at her apartment, where she lived with her mother. To get to her place, I walked past the main square, toward the blocks of apartment buildings on the other side of Lenin Avenue. It was a Sunday morning and there was very little traffic, so I jaywalked to avoid the urine and body odor smells of the underground pedestrian walkway. Normally Lenin Avenue was filled with buses, trams, and cars, and it intersected with an equally busy road, so on weekdays the underground walkways in both directions were necessary, for my own safety as well as for the unhampered flow of traffic. And as a full-frontal introduction to the city, the walkways were also interesting: lined with turned-over boxes and wobbly tables on which people sold copies of the local newspapers and the Russian version of *Cosmo*; prolific amounts of pornography in Russian, English, and German; pirated tapes; CDs and videos; sunglasses and watches; new and used shoes; Soviet-style note-books of paper; and paperback crime novels. Inside the shade of the stair-well, beside the currency exchange booth, stood a small gathering of men in leather coats who were willing to trade for my dollars. Off to one side of them, the pensioners, refugees, and handicapped veterans sat on the steps, begging or selling personal belongings.

But the stairs and walkways were warm, and their smell overpowering, so that morning I risked the light traffic and just ran across the avenue. On the other side I walked up a quieter street, stepping briefly out of the way for two kids on rollerblades who were expertly maneuvering the patchwork of potholes, exposed cottonwood roots, and gaping cracks in the sidewalk. I eventually came to Olga's building, one of four that surrounded a courtyard of well-tended rose bushes and neatly pruned trees. Olga had told me which stairwell in the building was hers and I found the blue painted door closed but unlocked. Inside Olga's stairwell each light socket had a functioning light bulb and when I tested the elevator, it worked too. I took it up to the fifth floor, wondering who else lived in the building. Obviously it was a block of apartments for important people. Very few of the other buildings I had been in still had light bulbs in their public spaces.

When I stepped out of the elevator on Olga's floor and found her door, I knocked and waited only a second or two before an older woman opened it and asked me to come in. She introduced herself as Olga's mother while handing me a pair of felted slippers to put on. One does not wear outdoor shoes inside Russian homes, and most Russians will have a pair of slippers for their guests to wear while visiting. Olga was standing behind her mother, peeking through the beaded curtain which divided the entryway from the rest of the apartment. She smiled hello while I took off my shoes and put them next to the two other pairs of low pumps by the door. I set my purse down next to my shoes, but Olga's mother quickly lifted it off the floor and set it on the shelf, muttering about how dirty her floors were, which of course they weren't.

"*Ochen' priiatno poznakomit'sia*" (It's very nice to meet you), I said to them both and thanked them in Russian for inviting me over for tea. I handed Olga the box of chocolates I had brought with me. "Our pleasure," said Olga's mother. "We're honored to have you here as a guest, and we're really excited about the chance to practice our English." Her accent was a beautiful British-Russian blend, and her grammar was perfect. Olga nodded in agreement and when she spoke I quickly realized that they were both very good at English because Olga's mother had worked as an English teacher for over twenty years, though these days she was supplementing her income by doing housework for foreign businessmen.

They ushered me into the main room, which was as spotlessly clean as the hallway, and over to a small table that had been placed in front of the living room window. I could see that the apartment had a kitchen and another room, too, which made it fairly large for a two-person family. The furniture in the place was well kept but at least fifteen years old, and there were very few decorative trinkets or Western consumer goods in the apartment. On one of the bookshelves stood a framed photograph of a man in uniform that looked as if it had been taken in the eighties, and I suspected that Anya was the widow of a military officer, which would explain the apartment in a building that still had light bulbs in the corridors. It would also explain the sparse furnishings, since widows' pensions, hyperinflation, and the general state of teacher's salaries since the dissolution of the Soviet Union would not have left Anya and Olga with any significant income to count on, except what Anya could make cleaning. But those material items they did have in the apartment were in good condition and their hospitality was warm and sincere. I was given the chair looking out their picture window and Olga sat down at one of the narrow ends of the table. Their apartment was high enough up that I could see over the tree-lined avenue below. When we had sat down, Olga's mother told us to get started with the interview and excused herself to the kitchen to make the tea. Olga nodded obediently and pulled over the shoe box that was sitting on the table between us.

"Thanks for agreeing to speak with me," I said.

"Of course," Olga said politely. "I was interested in meeting you when I got your letter. I know a lot of other women who are doing this, too, and I want to know how many are successful, how many actually find a husband." She looked at me and for some reason I wondered if the red tint in her light brown hair was natural or not.

"I thought you might want to see some of the letters I've gotten," she said, taking the lid off of the shoe box, which was nearly full of neatly stacked envelopes standing on their bottom edge, like reference cards in an old-fashioned library card catalogue. It felt like I was being shown a closely guarded treasure chest.

"That's a lot of letters," I commented, impressed. "Are they all from men?"

"Yes," she said seriously. "All except yours. But I haven't found the man I'm looking for, yet." She had started sifting through the envelopes with her fingertips, looking for a specific letter to show me. I watched her long, delicate fingers, which were as thin as the rest of her, flick each envelope back. Olga was relatively tall, maybe five foot seven or eight, but skinny, and fairly young. Her Web page had said she was nineteen, but that information dated back a couple of years because she was now twenty-one and about to graduate from the local teachers' college, where she was training to be an English teacher like her mother. Her blue-green eyes and the visible bone structure in her face made her strikingly beautiful, both in person and in her photograph on the Web. I was not surprised that she was receiving lots of letters.

She mumbled something about not finding the letter she was looking for but stopped anyway and pulled out a thin envelope with a photograph inside. She handed it to me. "I get a lot of letters like this," she said. "But I don't think that type of men seems very special, so I don't usually answer them. And most of them are from small towns, anyway. I don't want to live in the provinces. I have to live in a large city."

I looked at the photograph she handed me of a young man standing next to a blue Honda sedan, and I then read a bit of his letter. He was a twenty-eight-year old in the Midwest, and the first thing he wrote was that he thought Olga was very pretty. Then he told her he was divorced and had two children who lived with their mother, and he said that this time he was looking for a wife who was nice and happy. He asked Olga if she was like that. But she just shook her head when I handed the letter back to her.

"You didn't answer his letter?"

"No. I didn't think it was personal enough. It was so short, and he didn't even mention what I like or what I'm studying. He probably sent the same letter to lots of different women."

"Do they do that? The men? Send the same letter to lots of different women?"

Olga shrugged slightly. "I don't know for sure, but I think so. I mean, I don't care if they do, but I want to be with a man who thinks I'm interesting and who maybe likes the same things I do. I wrote on my application that I like opera music and am studying to be a teacher. If they can't be bothered to even mention who I am as a person when they write to me, then I'm not really interested in them."

She looked at the photograph of the man again. "A lot of them send me pictures of their cars," she said. "Why do they think I'd be interested in seeing that?"

I shrugged. "I guess they're proud of their cars? The type of car you drive is pretty important in America."

"I'd rather see a picture of their children," Olga said. She put the envelope back in the box and pulled out another picture and showed it to me. This time the man was standing next to a perfectly renovated 1957 Oldsmobile with a nice paint job and shiny chrome. He had written what kind of car it was on the back of the photograph. "At least that car is interesting," she said as she leaned close to me to look at the picture too. "But I didn't write to him, either."

"He probably sent you that one because antique cars are his hobby," I said.

Olga nodded as if she understood that already. Then she pulled out another letter and photograph of a thirty-something in front of a large red truck and handed it to me, as if to emphasize her point.

"Do all of them send you a picture with their letter?" I asked.

Olga shook her head no. "The English and the French don't generally send photographs of themselves right away, but the American men do. Most of the letters I get are from the US, anyway, including a lot from Alaska. But I've also gotten letters from Australia, Nigeria, Egypt, Italy, Spain, France, England, Holland . . ." She let the sentence drift off as if those were just a few of the countries in which her photograph had kindled interest.

I looked again at the picture of the bearded man in front of his truck. "You didn't write to him, either?" I asked and she said no.

"Can I read his letter?"

"Of course." She handed it to me and I unfolded the paper. It was handwritten, but not particularly personal. He talked about his job, installing garage doors, and about the truck, which he had bought recently. Then he told Olga that he was looking for a woman who was not a man-hating feminist. "American women are only interested in their own careers. I want a wife who'll take care of our home and children."

This reference to "American feminists," or "feminazis" as they were frequently called, was not to be the last one I would see in the letters women showed me, and it did not seem to elicit any surprise from Olga, either. Often the men used the first couple of paragraphs in their letters to explain why they were looking for a wife in Russia, and most of the reasons they gave could be boiled down to dissatisfaction with the women they found in America.

At first I found the vehemence with which the men discredited American women in their letters a little surprising, but it came up so frequently that after a while I stopped reacting to it. I could only assume they were responding to what must be a very frustrating dating scene for them. Obviously they were not finding the type of women they wanted to marry in America, and maybe they were not even finding women who want to get married to them at all. That this frustration was so universally blamed on the feminist movement was a bit of a shock, but maybe it is because marriage has come under criticism from parts of the feminist movement.[1]

However, despite the alleged difficulties these men encountered in finding a wife, and despite the fact that female-headed households are on the rise, marriage is still the norm for both men and women in most places.[2] And for women, aside from the intangible, emotional benefits of being in a relationship and raising children, marriage can provide other very real rewards. In some cultures, and in some places still in America, wives can expect to be sheltered, fed, insured, provided for, and to some extent protected (at least from violence outside of the home) in exchange for the "caring" work they do for the household. Marriage also gives a woman social status. And sometimes, for some women, these things are not as easy to come by outside of marriage. But as American society has changed and women have become more self-sufficient, as they have entered the workplace and it has become acceptable to be single, women are not as dependent on finding men to marry in order to create a decent life for themselves. They can leave abusive or unhappy marriages.[3] Or they can choose not to get married at all. For some American women, being married can lead to discrimination in the workplace ("she'll just end up having babies"). An American woman often (but not always) changes her name at marriage, unlike the man; and women still do a larger share of the housework, something that is often less valued than the man's financial contribution to the mortgage or car payments.[4] As many have already argued, the well-known phrase "I now pronounce you man and wife" places men and women in unequal positions,[5] which may exemplify fundamental reasons for women to avoid marriage.

It is possible that some American women are, therefore, deciding that marriage is not a goal worthy in and of itself, though I doubt it is as common a decision as the men's letters would imply. At the same time, every so often it seems as if "new research" comes out proving that married *men* live longer, make more money, and are happier, and so forth, than their unmarried counterparts. Likewise, movies, magazines, and TV tend to insist that "being in love" is the best way to be.[6] The statistical decline in the number of married couples in America could imply that finding a mate is more difficult for those men who are trying to "be in love," live longer, make more money, and be happier.[7] In any case, the "traditional" model of the household, with a father who works and a stay-at-home mother, is losing ground, even if it has never been as widespread as the stereotype would suggest,[8] so for American men who are trying to recreate that model in their own homes, it is inevitable, statistically, that at least some of them will run into difficulties. While the "decline" of the nuclear family may actually be due to structural changes in the economy and shifts in the social fabric, some men opt for a tempting scapegoat and blame the feminists for their difficulties. This note was sounded in many of the men's letters and some of the interviews I did later in the United States. Finding a nonfeminist wife would, therefore, appear to be a good solution for some American men.

Russia is a good place to look for that nonfeminist wife. Even linguistically, the Russian concept of marriage fits with a patriarchal understanding of the institution. The Russian term for getting married, *vyiti zamuzh*, means "to follow the man." The pronouncement of marriage in English defines the woman in relation to her husband, but the Russian phrase has her literally following him. The same phrase is not applied to men getting married in Russia. I interpreted the American men's letters I was shown as indicating that Russian women following behind their men were considered better than American wives, since they thought American women had been damaged by the ideas of feminism (and already had children, did not take care of their looks, carried a lot of emotional baggage, etc. The list of complaints was actually quite long.).

Criticism of feminism was well received by the women I met in Russia. It would seem that the general population has accepted the idea that the appropriate, ideal type of womanhood is tightly coupled with domesticity and the appearance of subservience, rather than the much maligned feminist position, which has been associated with women who hate men, children, and the family.[9] The Russian ideal of femininity requires a husband and children, which makes the threat of being an old maid painful, something my friend Natasha had experienced and Olga was trying to avoid. Feminism is not a popular movement in Russia; in fact it is hardly a theoretical discussion. It is so unpopular that calling a woman a feminist would usually be interpreted as a direct insult.[10] And I realize that feminism can also carry a negative connotation for some people in the United States, but I think this understanding is stronger and less challenged in the former Soviet Union than in America. The term seems to carry with it an almost pathological connotation in Russian, associated with the antithesis of womanhood in an essentialist discourse. The word also reminds contemporary women of the dictatorial, all-embracing ideology under Soviet communism that insisted women were the equal counterparts of their male comrades yet simultaneously encouraged them to be soft and feminine and assume their natural roles of wife and mother.[11] It smacks of unfairly conflicting demands. Women were, theoretically at least, liberated slightly after the Bolshevik Revolution, and the work of Aleksandra Kollontai has been cited as an example of how experimental ideas about gender and female sexuality existed in Russia and the Soviet Union during the early part of the twentieth century. Although Kollontai's ideas were never really implemented, Lenin's socialism improved the civil status of women somewhat by allowing them to keep their nationality after marriage, legalizing divorce and abortion, and creating day care centers and public cafeterias.[12] But this liberalization did not last. For example, while literature is not a direct articulation of social policy, the various incarnations of the famous Socialist Realist novel *Cement* can be used to show how early experimentation with gender roles changed over time and women were gradually forced to shoulder the double burden of worker and mother.[13] Early versions of *Cement,* which was a state-sanctioned novel about the revolution, present the female characters as the sexually liberated, "New Women" of the 1920s modernist movement. Later versions emphasize the importance of motherhood in conjunction with the responsibilities of the worker. These changes in what was an officially approved book mirrored, to some extent, public policy shifts. During the Stalinist era, divorce laws were tightened, abortion was made illegal, and the medals for women's special achievements in motherhood were instituted, most famously the Mother Heroine award (*mat' geroinia*), which was given to women who bore ten children.[14]

During the 1950s the Soviet government declared that women's emancipation had been achieved, and photographs of women wearing hardhats, driving tractors, and working in factories were regularly published.[15] And on paper at least, despite the Stalinist backlash, the communist state did do much for gender equality: abortion rights were reinstated;[16] women could get an education; they were allowed (or forced) into the public sphere, politics, and the workplace; they were granted much longer and better-paid maternity leaves than many of their Western counterparts and guaranteed a job when they came back from caring for their child; and the state-sponsored child care allowed them to combine motherhood and working life.[17] But these benefits—the health care, child care, educational facilities, and job opportunities—seldom lived up to their propaganda-fed reputations in the West. For the women who were forced to rely on them, their promises of emancipation rang hollow.[18] And the fact that these institutions were part of plan economies that did not truly address the needs of women was pointedly displayed by the fact that one could not rely on finding basic (feminine?) necessities in the shops,[19] and that birth control methods other than abortion were almost nonexistent. This state-sponsored emancipation gave feminism a bad name. As the Russian feminist Valentina Dobrokhotova said, "Equality is not simply giving women the right to shovel manure."[20] But that is what it seemed to do for many women.

Legislated gender equality, however hollow it rang, also affected Russian men. Some people theorize that anxieties about liberated female sexuality led to the backlash during Stalinism and forced women to return to the maternal, domestic role. Simultaneously, this created a patriarchal masculinity that also forced men into a narrow masculine identity, albeit one that offers them various privileges. These two very different yet complementary roles solidified the Russian sexual hierarchy,[21] a hierarchy which the American men access and take advantage of when they search for Russian brides with "traditional" values.

At the end of the Soviet period, during perestroika, motherhood was lauded again, this time by Gorbachev, but his was not the only voice encouraging women in the post-Soviet era to return to the home.[22] In the breakaway republics, ideas of ethnic nationalism emerged which were tightly coupled to conservative images of the traditional societies before communism. Women were cajoled to take up the precommunist and premodern roles of these idealized cultures while simultaneously shouldering responsibility for the family and future citizens, even though in truth many of these countries had been made up of agricultural cultures before being incorporated into the USSR, cultures in which women worked alongside men in the fields. But at independence, modern social problems were tied to women's participation in the workplace and they were told to return to the home.[23]

As Suzanne La Font notes in her study of women in postcommunist states, telling young women to stay home and have children kills two birds with one stone: it keeps them out of the workplace, which was and is suffering from cutbacks and unemployment, and it addresses the problems of falling birthrates and a declining population.[24] If women can see returning to the hearth as an actual choice, then it sometimes appears to them to be a better option than being forced into the workplace like the older generation of women had been under communism. It is interesting to note, however, that when it comes to mail-order brides, one of the sites claims that Russian brides may want to stay home the first couple of months after moving to America, but they will soon get bored and want to get a job.[25] And regardless of whether the woman is in Russia or in America, it ought to be clear that having the real *choice* to do either is the truly liberating situation. Because even if some women feel that perestroika's emphasis on women's role as mother and homemaker was more fitting to their true nature than being forced to be a worker, in both cases women were not actually given the right to decide for themselves what role they wanted to take.[26] And perestroika's rhetoric about women returning to the home ignored the fact that for most Russian households the woman's paycheck was and is an economic necessity, and that many women take pride in their work and would continue to work even if their husband earned a "family wage."[27] This last point explains why many of the women I met said they would try to find work in America, though they did not want to pursue a career. Olga, for example, said she was planning to work, but in a way that combined her job with being a mother. This came up after she showed me the letter from a man she *had* written back to, a thirty-four-year-old with two children who was looking for an antifeminist to help him raise his kids.

"Would you want to take care of his home and children?" I asked Olga, gesturing to the letter I was holding.

"If I married him, of course. That's what all women want."

"What kind of social life do you think you'd have? Where are you going to make friends?"

Olga nodded as if she understood what I was trying to ask. "I don't know. I worry about that sometimes. Of course, my husband will be my closest friend. And I'm sure my husband's friends will be my friends. And I'll make friends at work."

"You see yourself working?"

"Yes. I'm going to be a teacher." She said this as if I had forgotten that she was studying at the teachers college. "I wouldn't want to be entirely dependent on my husband and I don't want to just sit around at home."

"But if your husband doesn't want you to have a career?"

"I don't want a career. I'm not a feminist. My family will be my first priority, but I do want to have a job and make some money."

"And what if your husband doesn't want you to work?"

Olga looked at me as if she didn't think that would happen, but then she shrugged. "Well, in that case we'll have to talk about it and compromise."

Nearly all the women I met envisioned working outside the home as part of their new life as an American wife, even though they vehemently denied being feminists. This is not necessarily the contradiction it may appear to be. The contexts in which Western feminism has developed have been so different from the life Russian women have led that the debate about whether or not one is a feminist becomes pointless. Certain goalposts of Western feminism, like the right to full-time employment, appear ridiculous to Russian women who were forced into the labor market under communism but still required to shoulder domestic responsibilities.[28] Perhaps because of this experience, the idea of not holding a job at all is also foreign to them. Even the basic issue of universal suffrage can draw tired, cynical smiles from women in Russia, since women had the right to vote in the Soviet Union, but their votes did not make much difference.[29] And other issues that feminism in the West has tackled, like the right to legal abortions, seem equally ludicrous to a population which has long been forced to rely on abortion as a method of contraception. While reliable statistics are hard to come by, and estimates vary, the average Russian woman in the mid-1990s had somewhere between three and fifteen abortions during her lifetime, often without anesthesia and without particularly sympathetic care from the medical profession, because she has no other choice of reliable, affordable birth control.[30]

The reality of this statistic struck me when I saw a close friend encounter the Russian women's clinic. This happened when I was studying in Russia. It was 1994. I was living in a one-room apartment and I had just come home from an afternoon class. As I was unpacking the loaf of rye bread and the bottle of black currant jam I had picked up, there was a knock at my door. A muffled voice called out, "It's Oleg," the way Oleg and his wife always announced themselves when they came to visit. I had not been expecting them. Russian friends had a way of just dropping by, but they lived in the center of town, so it was unusual that they would travel all the way out to my region unannounced. They had a room in one of the university's dorms, sharing eighteen square feet of married student accommodation with a desk that doubled as a table, a hot plate, and a bag of perishables hung out the window to keep cold. The dorm had one toilet on each floor and a single bare pipe that dripped hot water in the basement and served as a shower for the hundred or so students who lived there. Because of this, Lena and Oleg would usually come by once a week and shower in my apartment. But they usually did not show up in the middle of the afternoon. I went to the door thinking it was lucky I had the bread and jam to serve with tea.

When I opened the door, though, only Oleg was there. He and Lena were almost inseparable, in a marriage that reminded me more of the camaraderie preteen girls can develop than the other Russian marriages I had seen. They were actually best friends. They shared everything with each other and had been a team since they left home as fifteen-year-olds. So as soon as I realized that Lena was not there and saw Oleg's worried eyebrows, I knew something must have happened to her.

"Lena's in the women's clinic," he said. "She miscarried early this morning."

I had been unaware that Lena was even pregnant. I knew she had been dreaming of having a baby, but I assumed they were waiting until they were better off financially. Lena and Oleg lived on his student stipend and the small amounts of dried peas and beans their families occasionally sent. The two of them were thin as reeds and seemed to always be getting over a slight cold. They constantly looked as if they were in need of a solid meal. I didn't think Lena's body was strong enough for a pregnancy. Apparently it wasn't.

Oleg said that when they had gone to the clinic that morning, they were told that Lena would have to have a D and C, the standard abortion method used at the clinic and one performed many times each day. But they were also told that there was no free anesthesia at the moment, either for miscarriages or abortions. Then they were given the chance to buy a dose for twenty U.S. dollars, a fortune they would never have been able to scrape together. So even though it was obvious that he felt uncomfortable asking, Oleg had come to my apartment to see if I could help them. I wondered how long he had been waiting outside for me to come home, since it was already three in the afternoon, but I didn't ask. I just grabbed my wallet, a few disposable needles, and a bottle of over-the-counter painkillers I had brought from America. Then we rushed off to the clinic.

I took the tram past the women's clinic each day on my way to the university, and I had seen women outside it on warmer days, slowly walking back and forth in the floral, cotton dressing gowns which seemed to be the standard uniform for a longer stay in the hospital, but I had never been inside. Oleg led the way up the clinic's cracked sidewalk and through its door, into a gray and blue waiting room that was kept cold by the painted concrete floor. There were five or six women sitting on chairs along the edge of the room, waiting for the nurse to process them. Oleg was the only man in the room. He had already waited in line once that day, so instead of standing in the queue he went directly to the receptionist and asked politely if he could pay for Lena's painkillers now.

"*Net*," the receptionist said, hardly even looking up. "Your wife has already had the procedure. You can go in and visit her if you like."

Oleg's face fell but he thanked the woman and we went through a double door, into the corridor behind the waiting room. It, too, was painted in a gray-blue color and was colder than comfortable. To our left was a large recovery room, filled with old iron frame beds that had at one time been white. Each bed was occupied by a patient. To the right was another swinging door into the operating room, from which I could, literally, hear women screaming. Other women were wandering aimlessly around in the hallway, in their floral gowns and slippers, though they kept to the edges of the corridor to stay out of the way of the steady stream of patients being escorted into the operating room. And everyone made room for the women who were being led out from the swinging door, women bent over in pain and walking only because the nurse they were leaning on was moving forward and they had to keep up with her or fall over where they were left.

Suddenly Oleg dashed forward and helped support a woman who was being led right past us. He had recognized her immediately, but it took me a couple of seconds to realize that the woman in front of us was Lena. She was wearing a colorful floral dressing gown like everyone else, but her face was a pasty gray and twisted in pain. Both her hands were gripping her abdomen, and when the nurse saw that Oleg was there to take over she told him gruffly which bed to put her on and then went back into the operating room, barking at one of the meandering patients in her way.

Oleg took Lena by the shoulders and led her through the corridor to the recovery room. I was not allowed inside there, so I just gave him the painkillers, which I knew would be pitifully insufficient, and left to go back home. Lena was allowed to stay in the clinic for two days and Oleg was with her as much as possible, and when I met her after she came back home she was sad about having lost the baby though determined to try again. I attempted to be encouraging and supportive, but I wondered to myself why she would want to bring a child into a society whose medical profession had just treated her with such distanced and cold apathy. I wondered why she would want to give her community another life when the people charged with her care were seemingly so uninterested in the lives they had already been given. If Lena's future child was a boy, it would be lucky enough to avoid being a patient at one of Russia's women's clinics, but if it was a girl I wondered what Lena would say to prepare her for the confrontational disdain with which her reproductive health needs would eventually be insufficiently met. One thing I was sure she would not say was that a feminist movement was necessary to change the situation.

Despite the horrible circumstances Russian women are placed in, describing actions to change them as "feminist" is unpopular. But to some extent this is a matter of terminology. For example, as negatively as feminism is viewed in Russia, its counterpart, the concept of women's solidarity, is very strong,[31] both politically and in daily practice. The term "feminist" is an insult but many women are comfortable professing solidarity with other women.

This confusion over terminology seemed to feature in the interactions the women I met had with Western men. One thing I noticed throughout my interviews and the letters I was shown was that the term "feminist" was understood very differently by the Russian women and the American men who were using it. In the men's letters, I detected a feeling of contempt for feminists that matched the intensity the Russian women felt, but it appeared as if American men were applying it to women who had been contaminated, misled, or changed. For example, one man wrote, "My first wife became a feminist and was only interested in her career, not our children." In this usage, a feminist was something a woman became, a label for a belief structure and pattern of behavior. But to the Russian women, feminism seemed more pathological, a term used for women who were psychologically disturbed or physically deformed, and thus unfeminine in their biological being. Their distain for feminism, of course, could be related to the top-down imposition of "women's equality" during the Soviet era. But this does not explain the difference between thinking of a feminist as something one becomes versus something one is.

The women I spoke with tended to create a binary opposition between being a woman and being a feminist, as if a feminist could not be a woman and true women could not be feminists. This binary opposition manifested itself in comments like the one Valentina (see chapter 4) made: "We're not feminists. We want to be *women*. We don't want to drive military airplanes." The idea that a woman is a biological being, different from men and essentially connected to the act of childbearing, has been reinforced in official Soviet literature. Academic research on Soviet women notes this, citing, for example, official literature for newlyweds from the 1970s which stated that "pregnancy and child birth are essential for a woman's organism. . . . After giving birth a woman begins to live life more fully. Women with many children usually look younger for their age, are more energetic and healthier than those who have no children."[32] It has been asserted that, to be an adult female fully integrated into Russian society, one must be a married (or divorced) woman with a child. A childless or never married woman is not accorded the respect given to her maternal counterpart and is not allowed to participate in society as an entirely "normal" woman.[33] To be a woman is to be a mother.

This discourse conflates sex and gender and encourages childbearing in a country that has had persistently low birthrates. It comes from propaganda which suggests that womanhood is related to biology. But it does not necessarily equate feminism with the antithesis of womanhood. Why this is the case is more complicated. The Soviet push to liberate women (or at least bring them into the workforce) did not parade under the name "feminism," and there was not a grassroots feminist movement to speak of during the Soviet period, either. So it is possible that associations attached to the term still stem from the way it was used before the 1917 revolution. At that time, the Russian intellectual community was heavily influenced by German thought, and in Germany around the turn of the last century, women who supported feminist ideas like the right to vote or study at the university were sometimes labeled *Mannsweiber* (male women) or *invertiertes Geschlecht* (inverted sex), terms that refer to biological aspects of an individual's identity.[34] Perhaps these ideas continue to lurk in the background of the Russian understanding of feminism. That would explain why the term "feminism" is so universally associated with lesbianism in Russia, both in public and academic discourse.[35] By emphasizing the fact that they are not feminists, the women are making the point that they are heterosexual.[36] And while feminists are sometimes conceived of as masculine or lesbian in America,[37] as well, there seemed to be less of this in the men's letters than in the comments of the women I met. This difference in how the American men and Russian women perceived feminism is particularly interesting given that many of the older women I met during my research were employed full time, adeptly running their lives on their own, and had a fairly disdainful tone when they spoke about Russian men, something that could be akin to the "man-hating" sentiments of feminists that the American men were trying to escape. Yet these same women vehemently denied being feminists.

It also struck me as a little problematic that the method these women were using to try to take control of their future involved binding their destiny to another person, to a husband, yet none of them mentioned the lack of control and self-determination such a relationship could potentially involve. To them, a discussion about the power aspects of a traditional marriage structure seemed to be unnecessary, again generally associated with Western feminism.[38] But seen from their perspective, they had a point. The potential influence one man could have on one's life and future could seem trivial compared to the overbearing dictates that the social structures of the former Soviet Union currently have on their lives. And perhaps they had not really thought about the degree to which they would be dependent on their husbands for daily support and social integration into the new society, as well as for their official status as legal residents in the new country.

But—to return to my interview with Olga—before I could initiate a discussion of how she defined a feminist, and before we could talk more about the expectations some men had of wives who did not work outside the home, her mother came out with the tea and a tea kettle of boiling water. She poured me a cup, expertly combining the concentrated tea and the hot water in midstream to make a perfect blend. Then she made sure I saw that there was sugar on the table if I wanted some while pouring a cup for Olga and for herself. She took the water back to the kitchen and returned with a plate of Ritz crackers and chocolates. I knew the Ritz crackers in the import grocery store were very expensive and felt a little guilty that they had been brought out for my visit. After Anya sat down and we had sipped our tea, I looked at her and Olga and asked why they had decided to list Olga on the Internet.

"I had two friends who were already doing it, and they encouraged me," Olga said, placing herself in the same category as many of the other women I met. Most of the women have a friend or an acquaintance who has "found love" through the mail, even though the women do not always tell many people that they are writing to Western men, at least not until they have really found success. There is a slight double standard here. Writing to men this way can sometimes be perceived as admitting the women are not able to find a Russian husband,[39] admitting they are at risk of becoming an old maid like Natasha, who was unmarriageable at twenty-three. And not all, in particular Russian men, are enthusiastic about their fellow countrywomen leaving Russia for American or European husbands. The Russian press has run warning stories about jilted Russian boyfriends who have managed to make their girlfriends' lives difficult even in America. Likewise, in some circles, dating a foreigner is seen as "selling oneself for money."[40] So the women usually keep what they are doing somewhat quiet until they find a husband. At the same time, there are a lot of women who list themselves on the Internet, and even those who don't generally claim that it is an understandable and viable option for young women.[41] And while women may not tell everyone they know about their correspondence, many of the women do share their letters and experiences with their close friends and neighbors, so it is not seen as particularly taboo.

"But actually, it was when we saw what happened to our neighbor, Katya, that we decided to try this for Olga. Wasn't it?" Anya directed her answer half to me and half to Olga, who nodded in agreement.

Olga's mother told me about another woman in their building, Katya, who they knew had been listed on the Internet. She had received a fair amount of mail and about three years ago had received a letter from an American man of Korean descent. Katya had initially dismissed the letter and not even bothered to answer it. "If she had wanted to marry an Asian man, she wouldn't have been writing to Americans," Olga told me. But this man was not easily discouraged. He continued to send her letters and photographs of himself and his life in Oregon. Then he started sending her poetry, both well-known poems and poems he wrote himself just for

Katya. Finally Katya wrote back to him, and as soon as she did he called her on the phone. Within a month he had convinced her to let him come and visit. When he arrived, other people in their building, including Olga and Anya, could not believe that Katya would consider seeing someone who looked so obviously Asian. But Katya not only met with him, she fell in love. Shortly thereafter she moved to Oregon, and, according to her mother, who still lived in the building, she was living the American dream. They had seen photographs of Katya with her small child in front of a suburban American house. "It's really wonderful," said Olga. But then she added, "Though, I don't know if I'd have answered his letters like she did."

Anya nodded in agreement. "So we decided to try to find the same sort of luck for Olga. Because there is no future for her here."

"But you wouldn't answer a letter from an Asian man, even if he was American?" I asked Olga, trying to press her on the point.

Olga shook her head no, but her mother corrected her. "Maybe you would," she said, "if he seemed really nice. Katya is very happy."

"Yeah, maybe," Olga reconsidered.

"Would you answer letters from a black American?" I asked her.

This time both of them shook their heads no. "I want to have children," said Olga.

"And you wouldn't be able to have children with a black man?" I sipped my tea, trying to make the question sound as neutral as possible but slightly disturbed by what I interpreted as blatant racism, especially since another woman I had met had said nearly the same thing earlier.

"No, I think we would be too different. I'm sure there would be problems."

"What kind of problems?" I wanted her to clarify whether she actually meant that she thought mixed-race children would be biologically problematic or if she was just alluding to cultural differences, though there were bound to be cultural differences between her and any American man, regardless of his race. But all I got was just an assurance that she thought having children with a black man would be a problem.

"You don't think there would be problems if you married a white American and had a child with him?" I asked.

"No," she said. "I don't think so."

The racism which I thought I detected in Olga's criteria for men was not something unique to her or her mother. Many of the other Russian women I interviewed underlined that they were interested in "European" men, a term I took to mean Caucasian, since they applied it to white American men too. This interest in marrying only within their race applied as well to potential matches they may have made with local men, something which has also historically been the case in the Soviet Union. The official line during Stalinism was that the archetypal Soviet socialist person was a racial hybrid,[42] but despite years of official propaganda promoting internationalism and the unity of the Soviet, intermarriage between races within the Soviet Union did not occur that often.[43] In the 1960s, a Soviet study had showed that the few intermarriages which existed in the ethnically diverse republics tended to result from men having studied or done their military service in Russia, married Slavic women there, and then moved back to their homeland with the woman.[44] Otherwise Russians tended to marry Russians, even when living in predominantly non–Slavic republics, a trend which continues today. I saw very few mixed couples on the streets, and when I checked out the personal pages in the local newspaper, nearly every ad contained a racial signifier, whether it was Asian, European, Christian, or Muslim, about both the person who had placed the ad and the partner he or she was looking for.

"I want to marry a man who is Christian," Olga said, as if that ought to explain her choice. I suddenly remembered the prevalence of the word "Christian" on the women's pages I had seen on the Internet. I had assumed it appeared so frequently because it was one of the blanks on the applications forms, but now Olga was bringing it up unprompted along with the issue of race.

"So you're Christian," I said, trying to get her to elaborate.

"Well, yes. We're Russian." She looked at me as if I was a little slow to comprehend. "I want to marry a man who is European, too." It slowly dawned on me that Olga used the term "Christian" to signify Caucasian, and for her "Christian" was tied to nationality and race. She is not alone in using the word this way; it has become common practice in Russia and been encouraged by the upper hierarchies of the Russian Orthodox Church, a proponent of an almost biological Russian nationalism.[45] The former Soviet Union, and Russia itself, has a population that is ethnically, culturally, and religiously very diverse. There are nearly as many ethnic minorities in Russia as there are people who consider themselves "Russian," and even those who consider themselves Russian are actually made up of people who at one time belonged to separate ethnic groups.[46] But this has not stopped people from forming self-identities based on race. I started to wonder if the other women on the Internet who also described themselves as Christian on their forms were using the term as a racial signifier rather than an indication of an arbitrary religious belief system. I was pretty certain some of the men who were browsing on their pages would read that part of their description and interpret the term within a North American framework, taking it to imply religious beliefs and possibly a conservative view of family life rather than race. On the other hand, most of the women I met seemed to be subscribing to the distinct gender roles, the importance of the heterosexual nuclear family, and female domesticity that I tend to associate with more conservative American Christianity, so even if the women were not speaking directly about a theological belief structure, they were nonetheless assuming the roles that the American interpretation of the term was expecting of them. However, Olga's use of the term to describe her race or ethnicity made me suspect that there existed a significant cultural misunderstanding between the men and women occurring around the word "Christian," just like the misunderstanding over the use of the word "feminism."

Interestingly, some of the websites advise American men to tone down their professions of faith in their initial letters. One even suggests that the men not say too much about their religious views at first. It advises them to "say that Christian values are very important for you but do not go in depth. Ladies do appreciate Christian moral values, they just cannot follow them in everyday life. . . . Life in Russia is completely different. It's so bad that one hardly can believe in God and that such a mess could have been created according his will. A woman will change her attitude in the West, and will accept Christian moral values with pleasure and devotion."[47] This, in a context in which many of the women claim to be Christian, would support the interpretation that the term is being used as a racial signifier instead of a marker of faith.

On the other hand, even if there is a misunderstanding about the women's use of the term "Christian" and their desire for a white husband, it is interesting that the women's demand for same-race relationships actually matches up with what the men want. One survey of Russian women looking for Western men indicates that 85 percent want to find a white man, 10 percent may consider an Asian, and 5 percent do not care if their future husband is of a different race.[48] Fourteen percent of the women on the website which prompted me to begin this study explicitly stated on their Web pages that they were interested in receiving letters only from white men. Likewise, it has been suggested that racism also lies behind the appeal Russian women obviously have to the American market. Prior to the fall of the Soviet Union, most mail-order brides came from Asian countries. But suddenly, starting in the 1990s, men interested in a mail-order bride could get a woman who was willing to take on the domestic aspects of being a wife and mother, had "traditional" values, was loyal (or at least dependent on the man for her visa), feminine in the stereotypical meaning of the word, *and* white.[49] Whiteness is, however, constructed and very contextual; what is white is an elastic category which can change with time.[50] And even though the Russian women are white, they are still constructed by the websites and the men as other, exotic, and foreign. Likewise, the Russian women are constructing the American men as other, exotic, and foreign. Yet maybe this is part of their mutual appeal. White American men and Russian women can find a partner who is exotic, but their children will still look like them.

That said, while ideas about race may in many cases match up between the American men and Russian women, there seemed to be a misunderstanding about the acceptable age difference between a husband and a wife. Older men look for younger women outside of Russia, too, as research on personal ads in the West has shown.[51] Several of the Internet sites for men, however, make the point that a Russian woman will think nothing of dating a man who is ten, twenty, or even thirty years her senior. Olga, though, seemed to think this was a little bit odd. At one point during our interview, while her mother had gone back into the kitchen to reheat the water, Olga pulled out a photograph of a much older man and showed it to me. She leaned in closer and lowered her voice.

"What is the average age difference between a husband and a wife in America?" she asked me.

"I don't know," I admitted. "Maybe five years? Maybe two or three . . . It's not uncommon that they are the same age, but I think men are usually a little older than their wives."

"That's like here in Russia, too," she said. "But a lot of the men who write to me are in their fifties. Sometimes I think they are trying to buy my youth."

At that moment her mother came back into the room and overheard what Olga said. She shook her head at her. "No," she said. "If that was true, then I would never have gotten a letter." Anya set down the teapot on a hot-pan holder and took a carefully kept letter from her apron pocket. She handed it to me and nodded for me to open it. The top of the envelope had been slit open along the crease, and from inside I pulled out a single piece of paper and a photograph of a weathered man standing next to a split-wood fence. On the other side of the fence stood a herd of cattle, grazing in a green field. It was bucolic and idyllic all at once, and the letter I read was honest and direct. In clear, handwritten English, the man explained that he was raising three teenagers on his ranch in Colorado, and he felt that he needed some help with his daughters and the house. He explained that he was writing to Anya because he wanted to find a woman with experience, who both knew something about life and about raising teenagers. Plus, he thought that the fact that she could speak English would be good. I looked up from the letter and tried to read Anya's expression.

"I applied with my photograph, too. This is the only letter I've gotten so far, but I had to write him back and tell him that I wasn't the woman for him," she said. "I couldn't live on a ranch. I need to be in a city. And besides," she looked at Olga, "I couldn't leave Olga here on her own."

Anya's reluctance to end up in the provinces is probably related to the attitude to life in the villages discussed by Elena Petrova on her website about Russian women. She writes: "The majority of Russian ladies seem to be rather cosmopolitan. The reason is that in Russia living in a small town or village is a nightmare. There are very poor life conditions, dirtiness, no entertainment, no goods to buy, even TV reception may not be available. Russian ladies do not know and understand the difference between small towns in Russia and abroad, and they just have this instinctive fear towards small towns."[52] To address their fear, she suggests the men write to the women about life in their towns, about what types of restaurants, cafes, movie theaters, and TV reception are available. She also suggests that the men mention where they can go for quality entertainment like the opera or the theater. Anya's suitor would have been smart to do this—though I am not sure how many of the men sending pictures of themselves beside a car or a deer carcass would be enthusiasts of the opera or theater or would plan on visiting these cultural venues with their new wives. Maybe Anya suspected this, since she was obviously taking care to ensure that she and Olga were somewhere that offered them a variety of opportunities outside of marriage, as well. Anya smiled at her daughter, who smiled back. "But," she said brightly to her, "you may not be here much longer, anyways. Have you shown her the letter from Florida?"

Olga shook her head and reached back into the box. She pulled out a peach-colored envelope from the very back, obviously one of the last letters she had received, handed it to me, and let me open it. Inside was a letter typed on matching peach stationery from a man who lived in Miami. (The websites recommend that men type or print their letters, so that the women they are writing to only have to struggle with the English language, instead of deciphering handwriting, too.) He began by asking Olga about her classes and explained that he, too, had studied at the university. Now he was working for a shipping firm and he owned his own house, but he had not found the woman he wanted to share his life with. He wrote that he hoped Olga could be the one for him, and that he promised to respect her and her letters if she would consider corresponding with him. The tone of the letter was extremely polite, and his grammar was correct, too, which set it apart from many of the other letters she had shown me. He had also enclosed a photograph, a professionally taken picture in which he was wearing a neatly pressed short-sleeved shirt and smiling, somewhat shyly, into the camera. I handed the letter back to Olga but kept looking at the photograph.

"Don't you think he sounds perfect?" Anya asked me.

"His letter is really nice, and so is his picture," I said.

"I think he's Muslim," Olga said in a voice that made it clear that would be unacceptable. I had not read anything about religion in his letter, but I was misunderstanding her cues again. "Look at his arms," she said. I looked at his arms, which had a fair amount of black hair on them. Nothing extreme, but they were hairy. "Don't you think he looks like he could be Muslim?" she asked me.

He looked like he could just as easily have been of southern European descent, but I shrugged my shoulders at Olga's question and said I didn't know.

"Well, we can write to him and ask," said Anya decidedly. But I could tell that Olga was not as excited about the idea. "We'll do that tonight," Anya said again. "We'll write him and ask if he is Muslim, and then we'll know."

"Okay," said Olga. "We'll ask him. Maybe you're right, Mamma. Maybe he is the one. And Miami is supposed to be a big city. I'm sure I could find a job there."

"If you move there and start a family, what language would you speak with your child?" I shifted focus to a practical issue.

"My child would be an American if it was born in the US, so I would speak English to it. Of course." Olga answered as if she had already thought about this. But Olga's mother was looking at her and considered what she had said. She was not as convinced.

"Of course you would sing lullabies to it in Russian," she said to Olga.

"I don't know," Olga answered.

"Of course you would," her mother said firmly. Olga took the hint.

"Yeah, I would," she agreed, and Anya looked relieved.

I sat and watched them come to their decision together, not wanting to intervene. It was not my place to come with advice, but it was interesting to observe Olga's reticence to confront Anya's determination. I wondered what Anya would do if and when Olga found a husband and left. It was hardly likely that she would follow Olga to Florida, or wherever she ended up, at least not at first. But I suppose Anya could always move to be with Olga later, once she was settled, and Olga would probably send remittances, like many other emigrants were doing. At that point, I had already finished my second cup of tea. It was time to go.

"I'll walk you down to the road," said Olga as I was putting on my shoes and saying goodbye to them both. So I thanked Anya for the tea and crackers, and for sharing her letter from Colorado with me. She smiled at the fact that I had remembered her suitor, and we said goodbye. Then Olga followed me out into the hall and down the elevator. When we had left her building and were standing on the sidewalk that led out of her courtyard, she turned to me and smiled.

"You weren't as scary as I thought you'd be," she said.

I smiled at her quizzically, "Were you afraid of speaking English?" I asked, thinking that might be what she meant. "Because your English is fantastic."

"No, that I thought would be fun. That's why I agreed to meet you in the first place. But I was afraid you might be one of those feminists that the men write about. They make it sound like every woman in America is a feminist, and I thought it would be frightening to meet one of them. They sound horrible."

"Oh," I said, a little confused. "Well, I'm glad it wasn't as bad as you thought it might be."

"No," she smiled widely. "You're not a feminist at all. You're very kind. It was really nice to meet you."

"Thanks," I said, thinking that the compliment was rather relative. It would have been difficult to live up to the descriptions of "man-hating bitches" and "ball-breaking feminazis" I'd seen in a number of letters. I thought briefly that it would have been interesting to talk a little bit with her about what characteristics the label "feminist" held, but I lacked the courage to ask. She had just said I was very kind, after all. How often does a person hear that? I didn't want her to change her mind. Plus, I had already taken up enough of her time.

"You are very kind, too," I said instead, and gave her a little goodbye hug. "Thanks so much for agreeing to be interviewed. And good luck with the letter to Miami."

Olga nodded and waved, while I turned to walk back to where I was staying. The traffic had picked up a little and I took the underground passageway, but I was too wrapped up in my thoughts about the interview to notice the smells. I was trying to imagine what it would be like to have a mother who was convinced my future lay in the hands of a foreign man, and what it would be like to think that myself. I had to remind myself not to jump to conclusions about Olga's ideas. Granted she would never call herself a feminist, but she was planning to work, and the fact that she and Anya were keen on making sure she avoided a life "in the provinces" could indicate that she understood her future to be only partly dependent on the man.

And as I walked back up onto Lenin Square I couldn't help musing over how strange it was to be labeled a nonfeminist just because I didn't come across as frightening.

3

Vera: A Catalogue of Men

I pushed open the door to the hotel foyer and stepped onto a worn wooden floor. In front of me was an old Soviet reception desk made out of wooden panels, and next to it was a wide stairwell winding up to the rooms on the second floor. On the right side of the foyer was a door that led to the hotel's restaurant and bar, from which cigarette smoke and vodka smells were seeping even though it was only lunchtime. On my left was a combination travel agency, information desk, candy and cigarettes kiosk built into a hole in the wall. It was here that Vera, who moonlighted as an Internet matchmaker, worked.

I introduced myself to the brunette selling cigarettes, and she turned out to be Vera. Smiling warmly, she gestured for me to come in through a door in the wall, next to the information window. She unlocked the door, set up the "closed for lunch" sign, and led me into a little room behind the kiosk that was stacked full of cardboard boxes of Marlboros and Lucky cigarettes, Snickers, and Twix bars. The room also had a desk and an extra straight-backed wooden chair in it, which Vera motioned for me to take while she sat down at the desk.

Vera had received my letter because she was on the Internet site as a woman looking for a husband, but she was actually working as an agent to help others get listed on the Internet. She told me she advertises her services, "Help finding international romance," in the local newspaper on the same page as the personals, but women come to her by personal recommendation as often as through her advertisements. For a fee, Vera works with them to create a winning application and to select which catalogues to submit their details to. She makes her money off the fact that not all the women who apply to Russian dating agencies get their information published on the Internet. One estimate suggests that only 15 to 20 percent of the women make it into the catalogues, and that they are chosen by the international agencies on the basis of age, beauty, children, and to some extent language skills. The addresses of young, beautiful women sell best,[1] and because the addresses are the product the sites are selling, it makes sense to publish those that seem most marketable. So Vera helps the women fill out their applications, both assisting them with the language, since most of the women do not speak English very well, and suggesting phrases to write under "personal characteristics" and "hobbies" which will be appealing to the men who are going to surf through the databases.

"When the women come to me, they don't know which companies they should send their photographs to, so I help them decide," Vera said as she pulled out a piece of paper with a handwritten list of companies on it, everything from a Spanish matchmaking agency, a German Internet company, several "flowers-of-Asia" sites, and the names of the most well-known American-Russian companies. I was not sure why Vera would be sending information about Russian women to companies specializing in Asian brides, but Vera explained that the women could choose any of the addresses and she would help them send off their application for eight U.S. dollars per address. Another agent I met with told me that she let the women choose which country they wanted to send their addresses to, instead of which company. That agent offered them a wide selection of destinations, including the United States, Canada, Germany, Australia, New Zealand, Belgium, Greece, Holland, and Denmark, and claimed it was easier for the women to decide on a country than a company they knew nothing about. She said that most of the women chose the United States or Germany. One of the women I met later, who had done this, explained to me that she didn't believe men in the United States were any different from men in other countries, but, as she said, "this correspondence is expensive, so I could only choose one country."

The decision to apply to one country, however, was not as limiting as it may have seemed to her. Nearly all the companies were Internet-based, and most were publishing in English, so the women's photos and details were available to a wide international audience. Vera's list of companies actually had a few non–Internet-based names on it, which she would agree to send a woman's information to for half price, but she strongly recommended against that. For one thing, she said, those companies produced paper catalogues that were usually black and white, the photos in them were small and poorly printed, and the personal information included next to the photographs was extremely limited. "And," she confided to me in a lowered voice, "the men who read those catalogues are usually blue-collar workers or prisoners. The men who use the Internet catalogues are more likely to be educated and employed."

Once Vera's clients have decided which company to send their application to, she helps them translate and write down their answers on the questionnaire about their personality, their interests, and the type of men they want to find. She showed me a couple of different versions of these forms, and it became clear that the questions on it dictated both the type and the format of information the women could give. For example, the women were asked to fill in small blanks with their physical characteristics, measurements, and educational and occupational status. To list their marital status, the women could check off a box for never married, divorced, or widowed, and there was a similar pair of boxes for what type of relationship they were looking for: a possible "marriage partner" or a "friendship/romance." There was a blank for the women to fill in their race, along with a set of tick boxes by which they could choose the racial types of men they would consider writing to: White, Black, Hispanic, Oriental, Indian, Arab, and "Does not matter."

Vera then arranges for a photo session at a professional studio in town, where the women will be made-up, dressed-up, have their hair done, and instructed how to stand, how to tilt their head in a coy way, and how to smile the inviting smile they need to solicit a response from the men who will surf their page. Vera told me that before she sends the women to the studio, she always stresses her number one rule for a successful application: Smile, smile, smile. "I helped one girl send off an application to a single Internet company and she had a wonderful, warm smile in her picture.

That girl got four hundred letters from *one* application." Vera beamed. "She's happily married in England, now. The smile is important."

I looked closely at the application form and Vera agreed to let me take one of them home. Then I asked her why most of the women she met were interested in finding a husband abroad.

Vera paused seriously at the question, folded her hands over the list of companies still lying on her desk, and said that there were three reasons women came to her. "Of course some of them want to improve their material situation, but women are also doing this because they are looking for companionship and understanding from their partner, and are afraid they can't find it here. Many women come to me and say that they want to try again, that they want to find love."[2] She looked at me to make sure I understood and then repeated the last reason. "They want to find love." I nodded at her and then wrote that down in my notebook. Her comment resonated with what I had heard from the other women I had met, and it had also been a major theme in the letters I received from the women I had written to. Many of them echoed one woman's explanation: "I have two children, am not pretty enough, and am not particularly well off. It is very difficult for me to raise my children, and I myself am not yet old. I want my happiness, and good fortune, if it is still there. I would like to try again." It was not only love but a second chance at love that seemed to be a common motivation.

Vera continued to explain that, first of all, during the twentieth century there had always been more women than men in Russia. This statistic is traditionally cited as a result of the large number of men who were killed in World War II, but life expectancy for men is also much lower than for women,[3] and Russian men are four times more likely to die alcohol-related deaths than women.[4] In the Russian population at large, there are about eighty-five men for every one hundred women, and because of the dramatically declining life expectancy for men, in the over-sixty age group there are only fifty men to every one hundred women.[5] Because of this, finding (and keeping) a Russian husband has been considered a challenge, though I had heard the excuse that "in Russia, men's population prevails" so many times before that I sometimes wondered if the rhetoric primarily served to explain away the inequalities, infidelity, and general misery that seem to pervade many Russian marriages, and to explain why so many children are raised alone by divorced single women. The second reason Vera gave for her large clientele seemed to be more realistic.

"Secondly," she said, "in our country we get married very early, and therefore we don't know the men well enough. But by the time we have gotten to know them, it is too late and so there are very many divorces." The average age for women to get married in the postcommunist states is twenty-three,[6] and even younger in the provinces. This can be compared to America, where most people get married for the first time in their late twenties and many wait even longer.[7]

"And thirdly, Russian men can't provide for the family, and they don't pay attention to their families," Vera continued, holding up three fingers as if to underline that there were more than enough legitimate reasons for her clients to look abroad. Vera's last complaint I heard from nearly every one of the women I spoke with. And it is true that those Russian men who would be starting their families right now are sometimes called a lost generation.[8] They are having a hard time negotiating the economic upheaval, social change, and not least of all the resulting unemployment. "That really doesn't agree with us women," she said. "Plus, they don't value what we do for them. And men in our county are prone to alcoholism." She added another finger to her list, as an afterthought. "So we want to try to find good fortune and future love in Europe or America."

Vera showed little sympathy when discussing Russian men, but by the time I met her, this did not surprise me. All the women spoke this way. They tended to paint a picture in which all Russian men had failed to uphold a bargain and, mainly because of alcoholism, women had been let down. They categorically criticized Russian men for being unacceptable husband material. When I tried to figure out what this was about, however, I formed a more nuanced assessment of the situation. I had to admit that the women's complaints were grounded in actual problems. Russian men do generally drink a lot more than men in Western Europe or North America. And many of them do find it hard to provide for a family. But the women's extreme dissatisfaction also seemed to stem from a sense of being cheated. Although it was never specifically articulated, the women seemed to think there was some sort of bargain made between a man and a woman concerning the roles each must have in a marriage. This bargain is built on the man's responsibility for being the primary breadwinner in exchange for the women taking charge of domestic chores. For an urban Russian male, apart from being the breadwinner, there are few other tasks he has in the household, except carrying out occasional repairs.[9] So if he is unemployed, or his paycheck delayed, or he is too burdened by alcoholism to hold a job, there is not much reason to have him around. The women, when they talked about this, seemed to see this bargain as completely natural and the roles connected to their biological sex. Surveys suggest that both Russian men and women are satisfied with this division of labor,[10] and as long as the men can provide for the family, this works. However, when Russian men are not able to meet the expectation that they will financially support the family, rather than renegotiating the terms of the contract, women seem to feel that they need to find other men who can provide for them and their families. The terms of the marriage contract in Russia, when it comes to domestic labor and financial provision, appear to be very rigid.[11]

This situation sets up a paradox within the gender hierarchy. Some people have asserted that within the Russian home the patriarchy is still very strong, and that "women are often grateful simply to have husbands who can help provide for the family and who do not abuse alcohol, let alone help with domestic chores."[12] At the same time, in the majority of cases the women are the ones who initiate divorce proceedings,[13] and many households with children are headed by women. So perhaps the stringent terms of the marriage agreement make for such an inflexible role for men, and one which has been particularly problematic during the economic turbulence and resulting unemployment since the dissolution of the Soviet,[14] that they are quickly becoming obsolete. Because the role of breadwinner is often the only one he has in the family,[15] and since family life relies heavily on cross-generational help from the infamous *babushka* rather than from the father, in the case of divorce, the father is easily estranged as a parent.[16] If he is no longer capable of being the breadwinner, he becomes in effect superfluous, and since domestic tasks are so strongly associated with the feminine, it is generally not acceptable for the men to take up these tasks when faced with unemployment or the inability to provide for the family.[17] Men who are unemployed are thus doubly excluded, from both the workplace and the household, and face extreme marginalization,[18] which can easily lead to alcohol abuse.

Vodka and Russia have come to seem like a natural word pair, and given the long history of alcohol abuse in Russia, one would think there would be social structures set up to deal with it, but this is not the case.[19] And in a country going through the upheavals that Russia went through in the 1990s, alcoholism is a risky disease.[20] It is not uncommon for people to freeze to death each winter after drinking so much that they pass out in the cold on their way home. And while in summer one may be less likely to freeze to death, the heat hardly offers a reprise. I remember one dead alcoholic I passed three days in a row during a hot spell in July. He was propped up against the wall of a building, in an alley outside the place I was staying. The first day he still had the half-empty bottle of vodka by his side, but that disappeared during the night, along with his shoes. The second day he was still there, and on the third he was starting to smell a little ripe. On the fourth day his body had finally been removed. When I commented about it to a friend she just shrugged her shoulders and said that the sanitation workers probably had not been paid that month.

Drunken men are visible in the streets and parks, at any time of the day, any day of the week. While there are those who have been left outside the social safety network and are more or less left to drink in the public arena, vodka is also a large part of the daily life of regular people. It is consumed in large quantities at parties, by both men and women, and in front of children.[21] It is easily part of any gathering of friends, particularly among students. And more than once, as I squeezed into the tram on my way to classes at eight in the morning, I smelled fresh vodka on the breath of the men next to me on their way to work. It really is as ubiquitous as the research, and the women's complaints, would suggest. A bottle of vodka can appear in the most incongruous places, at least to my North American expectations. I remember walking into an administrator's office at the university and finding it full of staff members all toasting with large shots of vodka at two in the afternoon. That was how they celebrated the eighth of March, International Woman's Day: the boss had brought in carnations for each of his female employees and then the office staff celebrated by getting tipsy and the men groped the younger women while toasting the beauty of their sex.

Even more out of place to my sensibilities, but apparently perfectly normal, was the bottle of Stolichnaya I saw during a stop on the Trans-Siberian railroad. Two friends and I had made it halfway through our trip from Vladivostok to St. Petersburg when we hopped off the train in Ulan-Ude. We had heard that there was a Buddhist monastery outside the town, the only one allowed to remain active during the entire Soviet period, and we were keen to see it. Despite it being January, it was not as cold in Ulan-Ude as we had feared. With the sun shining, and in our warm coats and fur hats, it was comfortable to walk around the town. We bought some stuffed pastries from a streetside kiosk and ate them on the way to the bus station so we could catch the next bus out to the monastery.

Determining which bus to take was a bit of a hassle, and the woman at the ticket counter inside the station was happy to sell us tickets but less inclined to actually tell us which bus we needed to catch. So we spent twenty minutes questioning the driver of each bus where it were heading and finally found the right one. The driver let us board, along with four times the number of passengers the stated maximum capacity allowed, and we three were squeezed into the standing-room-only area at the back of the bus. It was a little hard to breathe, but it gave us a panorama view of the trip. First we rode out of town, past the low-lying, single-story wooden houses with their brightly painted window shutters, and then for twenty minutes or so through snow-covered hills cluttered with parabolic antennas all pointing at different directions in the sky. We were riding through a military zone that would certainly have been forbidden to foreigners just a few years earlier—and possibly still was, though there was no longer any functioning security system in place to prevent us from taking the local buses right past the installments.

The monastery and its village were the final stop on the route and the driver was kind enough to tell us that he was driving the last bus back to town in an hour. We thanked him and entered through the monastery's red wooden gate into a garden of square Russian buildings with porches and roofs painted in Chinese red, green, and yellow, and with the turned-up roof corners normally associated with Buddhist architecture.

Three young American girls speaking Russian was a relatively rare sight for the other visitors to the monastery, and a newlywed couple who had also come out on the bus kindly took the time to explain to us what we should be doing while we were there. They led us around the interior perimeter of the compound, demonstrating the correct order in which to spin the prayer drums that were set up between the different buildings, and making sure we spun them the right way. They even tried to explain to us what was written on the different drums, but they had a hard time reading the symbols and settled on telling us the prayers were for good luck.

Once we had gone almost all the way around the monastery and were looking at the yurt that had been set up as an exhibition of how the people of the region used to live, our guide told us to quickly follow him inside a house nearby.

"I've convinced one of the monks to meet with you," he said, to our surprise. "They don't usually let visitors into their homes, especially women, but he said he'd show you his prayer room."

We followed him gratefully and stepped through the door of a little wooden house and entered into the main room, a small space no more than six feet by six feet, with pale red wallpaper. The floor had dark painted wooden boards, and in the middle of the room stood a desk, behind which the monk was sitting. He started speaking to us, but in what must have been the local language, Buryati, and the man we were with translated it into Russian. He first told us about the significance of his robes and his long, braided hair, and then he picked up a small handheld prayer drum, the kind on a stick that one rolls back and forth between one's palms to make the beads on its side pound against the membrane. He showed us how it worked and then he picked up the object next to it, a long peacock feather, and spoke about how it had magic powers as well. Then he said a chant, to which our translator listened and nodded respectfully at the monk when he was finished. We didn't get a translation of the chant, but our guide gestured for us to step outside. Bowing respectfully, we thanked the monk for seeing us and quietly filed out of the room, at which point our guide told us we had better hurry to catch our bus, so we ran back to the stop. Once we had started on our way to town, my friend Jenny turned to the two of us and smiled incredulously.

"Did you see the bottle on his table?" she asked.

We nodded and rolled our eyes. On his desk the monk had three things: the feather, the miniature prayer drum, and a half-full bottle of Stolichnaya. But he had not commented on the bottle. It seemed to be a part of the normal furnishings in his prayer room.

I thought of this while Vera was complaining about the problems Russian men have with alcohol. But she also brought up something that most of the other women had mentioned: the fact that age and children from a previous marriage significantly lowered a woman's chances of finding a Russian husband. I was a little surprised how categorical the women were in their characterizations of Russian men as uninterested in older women with children (and by older I mean mid-twenties). Granted, the group of women I met with could have been those women who would think that way, since they had already taken steps to find husbands abroad. But the frequency with which such comments came up is probably indicative of wider attitudes toward remarriage and stepfamilies, and of the roles men and women have in their households.

Within the countries of the former Soviet bloc, Russia has a disproportionately large number of women who are single, divorced, or widowed and also has the largest proportion of single-mother households,[22] which is partly reflected in the number of Russian women on the websites who have children. Yet despite the fact that Russian women are more likely than their counterparts in the other Eastern European countries and the republics of the former Soviet Union to form independent households, Russian women are also the least likely to receive paternalistic benefits, either from the state or from male relatives.[23] The extended family does typically offer some support financially in Russia. For example, it is not uncommon for parents to help their young-adult children, both during their university years and when they are starting new families, in much the same way as state subsidies and stipends do in Western Europe.[24] But child support after a divorce, as is common in the United States, is rare. Vera and the other women talked about this, and it is a topic addressed on websites for American men, too, who are sometimes surprised by the numbers of women willing to emigrate with a child. There are official requirements that the father must give permission for a Russian child to move abroad, or that the mother has the appropriate documents saying she is the sole caretaker of the child,[25] but there seems to be little discussion of the matter, indicating that bringing over a wife who already has a child is not usually a problem. One site, written by a Russian woman, explains the difference between child custody practices in Russia and those in other countries. "Children are considered to be a burden [in Russia]. Fathers often run away from paying maintenance, and use tricks like having two jobs and paying maintenance from the lowest paid one (in Russia maintenance is paid as percentage of salary). Fathers are rarely involved in the upbringing of their children from a previous marriage. They do not see them, not because women don't allow [it] but because they don't want to."[26] This is a very categorical statement, yet the interviews I did and the other research I read seem to support it. None of the women I met who had children were receiving any financial support from the fathers of those children. In theory, since 1995, both money and property are divided equally in a Russian divorce. But much of the Russian economy is cash-based, and many Russian women have as little knowledge about their husbands' actual earnings as the tax authorities do.[27] In addition, after a divorce there is often very little contact between the father and the family.

Vera told me she knew this was true from firsthand experience, and her discussion resonated with other women's comments. She claimed that many of her clients were in similar situations, and she used herself as an example of a larger pattern. "I've lived alone for five years, with my son, whom I love a lot. I've never been lonely. I've always been very busy with work, which often interrupted my evenings. All of my thoughts have only been for my son, and I never thought that I needed a man in my house. But recently I've felt that my son has missed being in the presence of a man, that he has missed the male influence. As a woman I give him a soft and tender upbringing. But he isn't a girl. And at the same time I've become a strong woman. I want to find someone who is concerned about me and even pities and protects me. In our country, men aren't strong enough to pity or much less protect women. They're often searching for such pity themselves."

Vera also added that Russian men were not interested in raising someone else's child, especially because of the way other men abdicate responsibility for their children after a divorce. A new man entering into the marriage would be expected to become the breadwinner for the child of the previous marriage, which she assured me was not popular.

She looked closely at me to see if I understood her situation, and then she continued: "I and the other women are writing to Americans because we want a man who is good, cares about his family, is happy and romantic. And attentive. And considerate."

"I don't know if there are that many men out there like that," I said.

Vera shrugged apathetically. "Of course I know that finding all those good characteristics in one man is very unusual. But my impression of men from the USA is that they fit those descriptions better than Russian men."

"Ummm," I nodded and made a note of her demands. In her first letter to me, Vera said she had been to the United States once to meet a man. She had been very reticent about discussing the trip when I'd broached the subject earlier in the interview, and although she had shown me snapshots from it, she discreetly removed all the photos depicting the man before handing them to me. She did not say why, but it was clear that he had not met her expectations. However, she obviously still held out hope for other American men. I decided to try to leave the subject of men for a bit and ask instead about how successful the women were when they used Vera's services. "If a woman is a bit older and has a child from a previous marriage, can she still find a husband in America?" I asked.

Vera nodded, and then she shook her head a little bit cautiously. "Yes," she said. "They can. But maybe they don't need to be completely honest about their age." Vera told me that when she first started working as an international matchmaker back in the mid–nineties, just about anyone who sent off an application would be assured of getting at least a few letters from men in response. But at this point there were hundreds of matchmaking agencies out there, offering thousands and thousands of gorgeous, Russian mail-order brides. "Beautiful eighteen–year–olds have flooded the market," Vera said. "And if they aren't eighteen, they still say they are. These days, if a woman comes to me who is a little older, maybe thirty, thirty-five, and especially if she already has a child, I tell her that I'll help her send off an application if she wants to, but that she should also consider looking at my catalogue of men."

At first I thought I had misunderstood Vera when she used the term "catalogue of men," but then she opened the top drawer of her desk and pulled out what looked like an overflowing scrapbook. This was her homemade catalogue of men. She laid it on the desk facing me and I opened it to the first page. Staring up at me was a photograph of a middle-aged man standing beside a smallish beige house. Next to the photograph Vera had written his personal details in Russian: his age, his job, how many children he had, and what kind of woman he wanted to meet. Below this information was the letter he had written to a woman named Oksana, a letter that started out in the first paragraph with a clear description of the woman he hoped to find.

Vera said, "The younger girls I work with aren't always interested in husbands who are over forty-five or fifty, but they still get a lot of letters from men in that age group. I tell them not to throw those letters away, but to donate them to my catalogue of men. They might not be interested in the man, but I have other clients who are."

I turned the page and saw another man smiling up at me. "Don't you think these men might be upset to know that their personal letters have ended up in a catalogue, to be read by lots of other women?" I asked Vera.

"No," she assured me. "These letters are definitely part of a wider campaign to find a wife. Look." She pulled out the letter from the page I was looking at, unfolded it, and pointed to the phrase "Could you be that woman?"

"Most of the men list the characteristics they're looking for in a wife and then ask the woman if she meets their criteria. They're looking for a specific *type* of woman, not a specific woman. So if I can help them find the right one by putting their letter in my catalogue, I'm doing them a favor."

I paged through the scrapbook, a smorgasbord of mostly older men posing in front of cars, boats, houses, BBQ grills, and the occasional studio backdrop. For the most part, their letters did seem to be addressed to "Miss Right-Characteristics" rather than "Miss Right," even if the characteristics they were looking for tended to describe what they did not want (a "bitter divorcée" or a "women's rights bitch") as often as what they did ("a loving mother to my children," and "a wife who will make a home with me").

"Do you want some tea?" Vera asked me. "You can look through these while I make some."

"Thank you," I said. "Yes, please." While Vera went to dump the old tea leaves out of her little teapot and boil the water, I further examined the catalogue she had so painstakingly put together. Her handwriting by each of the photographs was clear and careful and she had tried to present an objective and formalized description of the man, just like the women's Web pages I had seen on the Internet earlier. On the Web the women usually had at least two or three photographs of themselves, while in Vera's catalogue there was seldom more than one picture of each man. But the fact that the men had a whole letter in which to present themselves compensated for the missing visuals, and often these letters were several pages long. Sometimes the men adopted the self-description genre straight off of the Internet pages: "I am romantic, affectionate, sensual, lusty, loyal, honest, kind, generous, and tidy"; "I enjoy music, movies, tennis, skiing, swimming, biking, hiking, driving, nature and exploring new ideas, concepts and places," and many of the men were not shy about using nearly all of the space in their letters to talk about themselves. This seemed, to me, like a natural thing to do in an introductory letter, though a common complaint I heard from the women I had spoken with was that the letters they got from men were very self-centered.

Sitting in her office, reading the letters in Vera's catalogue, I felt as if I were being very impolite, and a little immoral, as if I were opening someone else's mail. At the same time, it was incredibly interesting. Here was the raw material that the women received in the post, the reason they had the image of American men (and women, for that matter) that they did. Most of the time the letters were written in very sincere and hopeful, if prematurely intimate, prose. Sentences jumped off the pages at me: "I want a wife who's loyal and family-oriented, and isn't a feminist like American women. Could you be her?" I picked up another letter that ended, "I look forward to the possibility of establishing a friendly and caring marriage with you which will grow, blossom and deepen into a journey of two entwined souls." The men were obviously thinking seriously and earnestly about what they were doing. And doing what they could to ensure that the relationship would work.

I unfolded a very thick letter that belonged to a kind-looking man from California with gentle eyes, long gray hair, and a neatly trimmed beard. It must have been the second or third letter to the woman who had consigned him to Vera's catalogue because he started out by thanking her for sending him the exact time and place of her birth. But then he went on to explain that the astrological test he had run against their births had indicated that they would not be compatible as partners. To support this, he had included a copy of the fourteen-page report on their incompatibility. Why Vera had decided this was relevant information to include in her catalogue, I'm not sure. But I found the seriousness with which the man was trying to pre-test the relationship charming, even if I suspected that his time and efforts would have been better spent learning Russian and trying to understand the culture of the women he was writing to, rather than consulting the stars.

When Vera came back and poured the tea for us, she commented on the catalogue that I set carefully back on her desk. "You can see what the men are looking for," she said to me. "They want a family-oriented, happy woman . . . children, maybe pets, and an attentive wife that is nearby, alongside him. And the women I work for, they can give the men that, and they just hope he appreciates and loves them. Doesn't a woman need that?"

"Does it work?" I asked her as I carefully blew on the tea to cool it down.

"*Da*," she answered emphatically. "In the last four years I've helped three hundred women send off their applications, and I know that fourteen of them have moved abroad to be with the men they've found. Of course, I don't know how it's gone for them once they're there, but I know they've found love." Fourteen out of three hundred is almost 5 percent, which is in line with what other industry insiders suggest the success rate is for Russian women using Internet matchmaking agencies.[28] And once the women move to the United States and get married, their chances of having a stable marriage seem to go up. One study claims that the success rate for international marriages is 80 percent after five years, whereas half of other marriages have already ended in divorce by then.[29] "But," Vera took a sip of her tea and became palpably more enthusiastic. "I'm working on a plan right now that will let me help even more women."

She went on to explain that she had heard that some of the match-making companies were organizing "romance tours" in Moscow and St. Petersburg, and she wanted to do the same thing in her town. These romance tours vary widely in length and price. They can involve anything from a week in Moscow or St. Petersburg for a few thousand dollars or visits in up to six different Russian cities for nearly twelve thousand dollars.[30] Room and board are included, as well as guided tours of the cities' cultural sites and several special socials or introduction parties where the men can meet eligible Russian women. Many of the websites about Russian brides suggest that the tours are definitely the best way to find a "lady."[31] They claim the tours save both time and money and give men a chance to meet many women in a very short time, sometimes several hundred in a week. The tours also let men meet the women face to face immediately, instead of after months of potentially wasted correspondence and telephone calls. The men are encouraged to pre-arrange a rendezvous with women they may already have been writing to, but it's not a problem if they haven't made contact with anyone before the trip: at the parties there is usually at least a five to one female/male ratio, sometimes up to a dozen to one.[32] Ideally, during the week each man will find a woman with whom he wants to develop a further relationship, and men are almost guaranteed to find several women with whom they can have a little "romance." At least that is the principle on which the romance tours are organized, though how many actual relationships grow out of the romantic encounters is unclear.

The industry sells these tours as putting the odds in the men's favor, but Vera was certain that this type of romance tour would also be a great opportunity for the women she worked with. From what I had heard about these tours, the women are generally so overrepresented at the socials that their chances of meeting a man are still pretty slim, not to mention the fact that some of the men who take these tours are not actually interested in long-term relationships.[33] And it would seem that the women invited to the parties are fairly well screened by the match-making companies beforehand, so older women using Vera's catalogue of men may not be invited after all. However, Vera was convinced.

On the other hand, as our conversation continued I learned that Vera already had some experience organizing romantic encounters in her city, so she probably knew exactly what she was getting into. She told me that part of her business came from arranging "companions" for businessmen who were traveling to the city and desired a bit of romance on their trip. She would find a suitable girl and meet the man at the airport with flowers, champagne, and a female friend for the duration of his stay. She told me about this as if it were actually a matchmaking activity, rather than an escort service, though I thought there was a difference. I felt a little unsettled by the way Vera categorized her escort service, her matchmaking service, and her dreams of future romance tours as part of the same activity. I was uncomfortable placing them all in the same analytical framework. As I reflect back on it now, I see what she was doing as an example of how mail-order brides (and husbands from her catalogue of men, for that matter) are placed together on a larger continuum between matchmaking and trafficking. Maybe this is a good idea, but there are important differences, stemming largely from the reasons a woman would employ Vera's services and the contribution the activity would make to fulfilling a woman's dreams of social acceptance, marriage, and motherhood. I know not all women have these dreams. But the ones I met did. I think their goals with the letters they are sending may be different from those of the escorts Vera was arranging for foreign business travelers, and the long-term goals of the men searching for a bride are probably different than those of the businessmen hiring a temporary companion. Pointing out this difference while still analyzing these two matchmaking practices as related issues on a spectrum of activities could allow for a nuanced discussion of the various phenomena, rather than the polemic the topic usually incurs.

These thoughts, however, took some time to formulate. Sitting there in her office at the end of the interview, with visions of her clients meeting men at the airport for a week of companionship, I wondered how it had gone for the fourteen women she had already helped find love abroad. Vera's escorts and the women whose bios she had sent abroad were not the same people, yet I was thinking of them together. That link which I made between the women who had moved abroad and the rendezvous in the arrival hall is indicative of the slippery discourses one often finds conflated when the topic of mail-order brides is discussed. And it is not always easy to hold them apart, especially when some people are active in both, like Vera.

4

Valentina: Searching for Companionship

I stood patiently at Lenin's feet, trying not to look out of place. Valentina had agreed to meet me on a Tuesday evening at the city's main statue. The day had been really hot, but it was cooling off as evening approached, so as I had walked across the granite cobblestones of the city square, I had scanned the kiosks along its edges to find an outdoor cafe with a bit of sunshine where we could conduct the interview. Meeting Valentina at the statue had been smart, since it was easy to find; the square was in the center of town, and Lenin stood in the middle of it, on a large, raised patio in front of a mausoleum-like building that housed the local Museum of Soviet Internationalism. The sun was still high enough that it was shining on the hat Lenin held in his hand, and the red marble of his podium both looked and felt warm to the touch.

I waited only a few minutes before a woman in her late thirties arrived. She had short, bleached blonde hair that was carefully curled and styled forward to frame her face, and she looked relatively trim. Her face was made-up, but not in the garish colors I had seen on many of the women in town. The dark browns of her eye shadow and the natural-colored lipstick gave an impression of reserved sophistication, and her skin looked smooth and healthy, indicating that she was probably one of the few women I had met who did not smoke.

"Valentina?" I asked when she approached me, resisting the urge to stretch out my hand. Each time I met women in Russia I had to consciously remind myself that shaking hands is a very masculine gesture there, and not something women do when they greet each other.

Valentina shook her head yes and then immediately apologized. "I'm sorry that you can only meet me, but Masha isn't living here anymore. She's been gone for over a year."

"That's fine," I said. "I'm interested in your experiences, too."

"Yeah, but it's too bad you can't meet Masha. She's the really interesting one. She's the one who's gotten the most letters *and* found a man."

"That's okay," I said. "You can tell me about her, too. Should we sit over there? I'll buy you a drink." I pointed to a small kiosk beside the entrance to the People's Park that had some white plastic tables and chairs set up outside. She nodded and we walked over and sat down. When the waitress came to our table, Valentina ordered a Sprite and I chose a Fanta. I asked Valentina if she would mind if I tape-recorded our conversation, but she seemed very uncomfortable with the idea, as had all the other women I met. So I put the tape recorder back in my bag.

"That's okay," I assured her. "We can just talk and I'll take notes." Valentina immediately became more comfortable and the waitress came back with our drinks, which made the mood lighter. Valentina pulled out a plastic bag of letters and set it on the table. I pulled out my notebook and broke the ice by asking her about Masha.

Valentina sat straight in her chair and folded her hands on the table. "First of all, you should know that Masha and I were doing this because we want to find husbands and we can't do that here." Valentina slid her bag of letters to the side of the table and went on to explain that both she and Masha had gotten married before they were twenty, and divorced before twenty-five. And just as Vera had posited, neither of them felt as if she stood any chance of finding a suitable man in Russia. Masha was pushing thirty when they sent off their applications, and Valentina was a couple of years older than that. She said that most Russian men were not interested in starting a romance with a woman that old, and Masha's situation was even more difficult, since she had a daughter from her first marriage. Valentina stirred her drink with a straw and said bluntly, "Russian men don't want to raise someone else's children. They are looking for free, well-provided-for and beautiful women," which was exactly what other women had told me. But listening to what Valentina was saying, I also heard another undertone. It was clear she did not think she stood much chance of finding a man who would be interested in her, but it also sounded as if she did not think there was any chance she would find a Russian man she herself would be interested in. Once or twice during our interview she mentioned the problems Russian men have with alcohol, and in the letter she had written to me she had explained that "Russian men, the majority at least, don't appreciate us, Russian women." Apparently her friend Masha thought the same thing, so they had started writing to men abroad.

Valentina carefully took the straw out of her glass and set it neatly on a napkin. I did the same, reaching for a napkin from the dispenser which, like most napkins in the former Soviet Union, had been cut along the fold lines by the thrifty owners of the kiosk, turning each napkin into four separate ones. I took a quarter of a napkin, put my straw on it, and kept taking notes while Valentina told me about Masha.

"Masha got lots of letters. I think she must have had at least forty or fifty different men writing to her, many from the USA. Some of them were not up to her expectations, and that's natural, as all people are different. But on the whole, the main impression we both had is that some overseas men are very strange, they can write one way and act absolutely another way.

"Anyway, she is still getting new boyfriends, even though she's been gone for over a year. We don't know how to get her photo off of the Internet, but Masha says that we should open her letters anyway and read them, just in case someone interesting writes to her. That's how I read the letter you sent to her."

Valentina had explained in her first letter to me that Masha was living in Norway and had been for a year now. But before she left, Masha had lived next door to Valentina, sharing a flat with her mother and ten-year-old daughter. I had a mental image of where they lived because I had gone over to Valentina's building a couple of days earlier on the chance I could catch her at home. Her apartment was on the second floor of a standard, gray, five-story building that must have been built sometime in the sixties. The architecture was typical of Soviet housing from that era and nothing about it differentiated her building from the numerous other identical buildings I had been in, both there and in other Russian cities. The outside door to her stairwell had been standing ajar and did not close tightly behind me; the row of blue tin mailboxes in the entryway was broken so that they could no longer lock; the concrete staircase was crumbling; and there were no light bulbs in the bare sockets. Valentina's hallway, which was floored with wooden planks that still had traces of orange paint on them close to the walls, smelled vaguely of cat urine, but the door to her apartment was sturdy, clean, and upholstered in leather, as were a number of the other doors on her corridor. I am sure the interior of her apartment was not nearly as run down as the communal areas of the building. She may not have had a modern refrigerator, since most of these buildings had a built-in cupboard under the kitchen window with a vent to the outside, called a Khrushchev refrigerator, but she almost certainly had running water and a wall-mounted gas heater for hot water. Judging from the placement of doors in her corridor, both she and Masha's mother lived in just one room and a kitchen, but even if they were small, all the Russian apartments I had been in were spotlessly clean and as well decorated as the owner's budget could afford. Valentina's apartment was probably sparsely but tastefully furnished and almost certainly felt like a home, even if she lived there alone.

She had not been there when I stopped by, and I later learned that Valentina spent her days working for the local newspaper. This was a prestigious place to work, though at the time we met, she and her colleagues had not been paid for two months. She was thankful to have a job, however, especially since she had been out of work a few times since her divorce. But she, like many others, dreamed of a future with more stability. Because of the educational structures established during the Soviet period and the economic situation of the region today, the women coming to America as brides are generally well educated. But then, so are most Russian immigrants to the West.[1] One of the other women who had written to me summed up their situation succinctly: "At the present time thousands of people, among them many with high levels of education and excellent specialist skills, are not necessary to anyone; the factories are standing still, industry is in a serious crisis, and there is very high unemployment." When I later met this woman in person, she told me that she was currently working in an open-air stand, selling imported clothing in the large bazaar that had grown up next to the train station—this despite her university degree in chemistry. "But there haven't been jobs for chemists here in ten years," she told me sarcastically. "I'm lucky to be working at the market." And she was.

The statistical material available about the former Soviet Union backs up her pessimism and her gratitude for having a job at all, as well as Valentina's. While not everyone is worse off now than they were fifteen years ago, the series of economic ups and downs, the periodic devaluations of the ruble, and privatization combined with the transition to free market capitalism (or robber baron capitalism, as some have called it) have left many people unemployed and others with wages or pensions that have all but disappeared in the face of hyperinflation. The gap between the rich and the poor has grown exponentially. In some of the former republics, the dismantling of the Soviet system has left between 80 and 95 percent of the population living under the poverty line,[2] and in Russia, estimates suggest that a fourth of the population lives in poverty.[3] Unemployment is rampant, particularly when compared to the full employment policies of the Soviet period. During the 1990s, women's employment decreased by 20 percent while men's employment only decreased by 8 percent. So not only were jobs lost across the board but women were crowded out of those jobs that were left.[4] Not everyone in Russia chalks this up to discrimination against women; many men and older women think the workplace is gender blind (or perhaps that the question is moot),[5] but surveys indicate that younger and better-educated women tend to feel discriminated against in the workplace because of their sex. The chemist I met did not mention this specifically, but she did say she was frustrated by not being able to use her chemistry degree. And she was not very satisfied working in the bazaar.

The employment situation for Russian women in the outer republics of the former Soviet Union, and even in some of the former countries of the Soviet bloc, can be even worse. The extent of the Soviet Union's cultural influence is still felt in many of the countries it had controlled. Bulgarian women, for example, share the same double burden as their Russian counterparts and also adapt the essentialist explanation that women are naturally better at caring for the family than men. Like Russian women, many of them sacrifice their own interests in order to nurture their family. Likewise, Poland has the same problems with official denial of (or disregard for) domestic violence, despite its prevalence in Poland's rural and low-income areas,[6] just as in Russia. But Russian women in the former Soviet republics have two strikes against them. The first is a growing feeling of nationalism that discriminates against Russians, who are associated with the old Soviet era. After independence many Russians have not been granted citizenship in the new countries, and even where they have become citizens, the state apparatus is to some extent now run by the local pre-Soviet population, so Russians have been squeezed out of jobs they once held. The Russians in these republics are becoming disenfranchised in their own country, in part because they often do not speak the local languages that have now become the official languages.[7] Yet twenty-five million ethnic Russians live outside Russia in the former Soviet republics. As these republics are becoming more and more nationalistic, life is more and more difficult for the ethnic Russians left in them.[8] However, the situation is complicated. The Soviet Union in essence colonized many of the countries it subsumed, and the "new" independence of these republics has initiated a process of decolonization. Russians living in these newly independent states may have been born there and their families may have lived there for several generations, but at some level they have always been colonizers, though this term has not always been applied to the Soviet Union.[9] There are those who feel that the colonizers should go back to Russia, and the price individuals pay in this political and economic process can be high. Nongovernmental agencies working in the Baltic States, for example, have noted a disproportionate number of Russian women, in relation to their representation in the general public, working as prostitutes in the capital cities, indicating their social marginalization as an ethnic minority and exclusion from the formal labor market.[10] When the Soviet Union was dissolved and migration became an option, many ethnic Russians in the post-Soviet states moved back to Russia (more than eight million did so between 1991 and 2000 compared with only one and a half million during the previous decade).[11] But unemployment among migrants in Russia is higher than average,[12] and perhaps therefore many ethnic Russians chose not to migrate, staying in the newly formed states. It would also appear as if migration back to Russia is easier for men than women, so not only are the women left outside the new societies being built, they are often left without much chance of finding a Russian husband in the former Soviet Union republics.

When in Russia and not part of an ethnic minority, women's gender still works against them in the labor market. There has long been and still is a distinct line between *zhenskoe delo* and *muzhskoe delo*: women's work and men's work, both in the home and in the job market.[13] During the Soviet era women were expected to work, but the labor market was still divided between men's and women's occupations, so teaching and medicine, for example, were distinctly feminized.[14] The gender division between different job sectors was reflected in pay, too, and women typically made only two-thirds as much money as men.[15] As the Soviet Union began its economic reforms in the late eighties, the horizontal structuring of the workplace along gender lines had negative consequences for women, since those sectors which employed large numbers of women, like education and healthcare, were steadily underfunded during the reforms. This meant that many women were let go in those sectors, and that the wages of those who managed to keep their jobs did not always keep pace with inflation. These changes started early on in the transition process (between 60 percent and 80 percent of the laborers shed during perestroika were women),[16] and have continued since, although there is some evidence to suggest that women may slowly be returning to the labor market.[17] That market is a very different place today, however, from what it was before. For example, whereas a teacher's salary in 1980 was 80 percent of the national average salary, by 1995 it had sunk to 68 percent.[18] And other industrial areas that predominantly employed women, like textile factories, were among the hardest hit by Yeltsin's reforms.[19]

As the health and education sectors have shrunk, the number of office jobs and commerce jobs available to women has risen. Even doctors, who in Russia usually complete their education and start practicing around the age of twenty-two, can be tempted to quit their jobs and work in kiosks and shops, since the medical profession pays so poorly in Russia.[20] This reality is mirrored in the online bios of the women I met, many of which stated that the woman had been trained as a teacher or a doctor but was now working as a secretary or selling goods in a kiosk or small streetside shop. More and more of these jobs, however, are being acquired through contacts,[21] contacts which some of the women I met did not have. And some of the jobs require services which would not normally be included in secretarial work. Vacancy advertisements for candidates who are "young, blonde, long-legged and without inhibitions" appear in newspapers, and some women have even reported being raped at job interviews.[22]

As if it were not enough that the women face job prospects which are divided into men's work and women's work, the market also actively discriminates against women.[23] According to the United Nations, women in the former Soviet Union are starting businesses half as often as men because of traditional prejudices against women in business. The effect this discrimination can have on economic growth becomes apparent when one considers that, in developed countries, women-led businesses are the fastest-growing segment of the small- and medium-enterprise sector.[24] For single women trying to make ends meet, discrimination like that is the last thing they need. I remember one discussion I had with a Russian businessman about a potential supplier we had met. On paper the supplier looked like the optimal partner, but the company was run by a woman, and that was enough to make him turn the opportunity down. When I asked him why, he looked at me as if I had missed the obvious. "Because a woman who runs a business is *nenormal'no*," he said. Not normal. For women, having a career (and not just a job) in the new marketplace involves somehow balancing contradictory identities of being profession-ally capable and being a normal woman, that is, one who is not interested in a professional career. Unfortunately, it is not just the private sector which discriminates against women in the post-Soviet workplace either; the Lithuanian Ministry of Transportation, for example, has openly adver-tised for female secretaries and male technicians, despite being an official department of a state whose constitution outlaws gender discrimination.[25]

The Russian women I met all claimed that they did not want a career, but it has been pointed out by others that it is hard for Russian women to want a career when they have never actually had the chance to have one, at least not in the Western sense of the word. The glass ceiling in Russia is so much more difficult to break through, and a woman would have to spend every day proving her worth as a co-worker, fighting against the attitude expressed by the Russian proverb "A chicken is not a bird and a woman is not a human being."[26] Not in the workplace, anyway. In such an environment, it is probably easier to accept the role one can shoulder respectably, that of mother and wife, that of "woman" rather than human being. For many women it is easier to be "normal" by just having a job, by just going into healthcare or teaching as Olga wanted to do, rather than going after a career in the new market-based sectors. But it should be remembered that, when the Russian women assure their American suitors that they do not want to have a career, they are doing so from within a culture that would harshly judge them as abnormal if they were to answer that question any other way.

Apart from discrimination, perhaps the most disconcerting thing for Russian women, and men is that the new job market is not a stable, rational market. Companies, banks, and the government can act in unpredictable ways. The term "virtual economy" has been used to describe the way much of Russia's business is conducted without cash, the prevalence of nonmarket prices, large debts, and wages that are long left unpaid.[27] I was personally confronted with this unpredictability as a student in Russia. One Saturday just after the fall term had started, I had headed out to the bazaar around noon to buy some vegetables. Most of the carrots that I could find in the state-run shops were large and tough-looking, but the *babushkas* selling garden produce in the bazaar had bunches of small, sweet carrots for sale. I went up to one of them, an old woman in a headscarf who had placed her carrots as the centerpiece of the vegetables she was selling on an upside-down cardboard box, surrounded by beets and a pile of potatoes. She must have sown the carrots late in the season because the green tops were young-looking. I asked her how much she wanted for them. Through her empty gums she lisped out thirty rubles, which I thought sounded okay, and since I had a really hard time bargaining with old ladies missing teeth, I nodded at her price and reached into my wallet for the money.

I had brought dollars with me to Russia because, although I had been told I would receive the same student stipend as any other university student, people had warned me that hyperinflation made it impossible to live on the stipends, which was true. The sum I got each month was enough to buy a week's worth of potatoes or heavily subsidized bread, but not enough to buy any of the vegetables or imported foods being sold in the open market. Every couple of weeks I traded some of my dollars for rubles, sometimes at the bank and sometimes with the men who stood outside the bazaar. Most of their business, and the bank's for that matter, was in trading with Russians who wanted to turn their rubles into dollars to guard against the rapid devaluation of the ruble in recent years, so everyone was happy to change my dollars to rubles. However, it had surprised me how picky they were. Both the black-market men in their black leather coats and the overly made-up young women behind the bulletproof glass in the bank refused to take any U.S. bills that were more than a few years old, and even newer ones were often rejected if they were slightly torn or rumpled. Having never experienced this type of mistrust of paper currency in the United States, I had not even thought about what kind of bills I took with me. Consequentially I had more than a few bills I was not able to exchange. What I learned, however, was that not all government-issued bills were worth what was printed on them. This became very clear when I tried to buy the carrots.

In the town where I was living, nearly everything was still being sold in rubles. The prices given in the official shops were in rubles. The price tags written on cardboard bits and placed in front of rows of Snickers bars and cigarette packages were in rubles. The per-kilo price for tomatoes and cucumbers at the bazaar was also written in rubles. Occasionally, if I would ask a question and the shop assistant heard my accent, I would get a dollar price and be encouraged to pay with dollars, but this was rare. This was not the case in many other places I had been. In St. Petersburg and Moscow both rubles and dollars were accepted, but dollars were definitely preferred everywhere outside of the older, state-run shops. In Vladivostok everything had been marked with both a yen and a ruble price, though yen or dollars were the currency of choice and kiosk clerks tended to protest when I tried to buy something with rubles. And in Murmansk, after having checked into a hotel that insisted I pay in dollars, I had gone into a store that specialized in imported food and they flat out refused to take my rubles. They had marked everything with prices in Norwegian crowns, and it took more than a bit of convincing to make them agree to let me buy the sandwich meats I wanted with U.S. currency.

Because of this polygamous relationship with currency in Russia, I was a little frustrated, but not too taken aback, when the old woman from whom I was trying to buy carrots refused to take my rubles. I had pulled out a twenty and a ten-ruble note that I had gotten from the bank earlier in the week, and after inspecting them a bit more closely than was usual, the woman told me that she did not want those notes. I pulled out a fifty-ruble note, but she did not want to take that one either. The only other money I had with me was a five-hundred-ruble note, and when I showed it to her she just shook her head no.

"I don't have any dollars with me," I told her in Russian, since I didn't and I was starting to suspect that she was trying to get me to pay with hard currency, though it seemed really odd that she would bother with that over a bunch of carrots. She just shook her head, though, and repeated that my rubles were too old.

Her statement confused me slightly. I didn't understand what she meant but I just shrugged, thanked her, and went a few stands down to buy carrots from another woman. The same thing happened with her, too, and I started to suspect that they knew something I didn't. I slowly left the market, wondering what was going on, and headed for one of the state-run shops before they closed for the rest of the weekend. I thought I could buy the older carrots anyway, cut off the rotten parts, and just cook them longer. The first shop I went into had no vegetables left, so I started off across to the other side of town, to another, smaller shop. On my way I ran into one of the other American exchange students. When I explained what had happened with the carrots, he nodded knowingly.

"I guess you haven't heard about the currency change," he said dryly.

"What currency change?"

"Apparently on Thursday the government announced that all old rubles would no longer be valid as of Monday. So yesterday there was a rush at the banks to exchange for new notes and to buy things in the state shops, which are still taking the old rubles. That's why there's nothing left in the stores."

"Uh-huh," I said slowly, thinking that was the strangest thing I had heard yet. The government announces on a Thursday that all old notes would be invalid on Monday. Insane, I thought.

"This country's insane," he said, as if he had read my mind.

"So the only place I can use my rubles now is in the state shops?" I asked, realizing that the banks were already closed until Monday.

"For the next fifteen minutes, anyway," he said looking at his watch. "After that they're closed."

"Right," I said. "I'd better get going." But when I made it into the shop I saw the long line of people, mostly old pensioners, who were obviously trying to do the same thing. So I just turned around at the door. There was no way I would have been able to make it through the line in time, and thankfully I had only 580 rubles in old notes. It suddenly became very clear to me why everyone I knew was constantly trading rubles for dollars and why they only wanted the new bills. I decided to swallow the loss, chalk it up to being in a foreign culture that I did not understand, and bring those rubles back to the States with me, along with the dollars no one wanted to take. That evening I made split pea soup without carrots and counted how many fresh-looking twenties I still had under my mattress.

For me, the experience was disconcerting, but exotic. I was, after all, just an exchange student and living off savings. But for women in Russia with full-time employment, a child, and sometimes a mother to support, bundles of dollars under the mattress are important to have. Those women who have managed to keep their jobs despite the layoffs have experienced long periods without pay even though they go to work every day. Sometimes at the end of the month, instead of a paycheck, they are paid in kind: a month's salary worth of sunflower oil, pantyhose, or toilet paper, and sometimes not at all. But despite sporadic and creative salary practices, most people keep going to work. "I take pride in being a teacher. It is an important job," one woman told me, even though teachers have gone for long stretches of time without pay. And aside from taking pride in one's job, employment, at least during the Soviet era, was much more than just a paycheck. It was not something one gave up lightly. A job gave the Soviet citizen the right to an apartment, residency in a city, child care, and a social identity. It has also been suggested that people in the former Soviet Union have continued to go to work each day because the culture of deprivation which existed for so many years under communism encouraged people to find individual solutions, like relying on food produced at their *dachas*, rather than organizing for better labor conditions and pay.[28] In addition, statistics suggest that it is easier for people with a job to get a new one than it is for people who are unemployed to reenter the labor market, which is another factor that works as an incentive to keep one's job.[29] Then, too, there is the fear that a bad job is better than no job at all, and many people cannot realistically expect to get anything else.[30]

Valentina's neighbor Masha was one of the ones who had kept her job. She had been working as a teacher before she left for Norway. But it had been hard to support herself, her mother, and her daughter with the salary she occasionally received. Now that she was living abroad, she was able to send money back home and things were a little easier for them. Masha's mother and daughter were still living next door to Valentina, and since Masha's mother could not read any English, she had asked Valentina to open and read the letters that Masha kept getting. When Masha called home, Valentina described the letters that had arrived and Masha decided whether she would answer them or not. "Actually, she doesn't need these letters anymore, since she's already found the right man," Valentina had written to me, but apparently Masha was not as convinced.

"Anyway, Masha's beautiful," Valentina continued during our interview as she sipped her Sprite. "And the photographs she sent to the matchmaking companies were very good, which is important. In fact, I think that's the only thing that matters, really, a good photograph. Everything else, including your age and whether you can speak English or not, is unimportant, as long as you have a good photograph. Then you'll get lots of letters, like Masha."

Masha had worked with a local agent to send off her photographs and application form to a number of companies in America and Europe. The agent charged her a small fortune, but her help had been worth it, both because the agent had the addresses of the Internet companies and because she helped Masha fill in the bio correctly. Despite what Valentina said about the photograph being the only important thing in the application, it was also important to get some things right on the bio. For example, it was no coincidence that most of the women's pages said that they were looking for a man who was "loyal" and "financially secure." But the male audience surfing the pages also had some desires in common, and Masha's agent told her that the men were interested in women who had hobbies like cooking and knitting and who stayed trim by working out. So Masha had written those terms down on her application. "Masha understood that the men wanted a real woman," Valentina told me, meaning a very feminine and docile wife. "But that suited us fine. We're not feminists. We want to be *women*. We don't want to drive military airplanes. We want to have a family and a good husband who can provide for his family."

The agent also helped Masha get those all important "beautiful pictures," just as Vera did with her clients. She had been sent to a photography studio in town which specialized in mail-order-bride pictures, where she had also been able to rent clothing for the shoot. The photographer had shown Masha how to hold her head and hands, and how to stand so that her chest and hips were accented and the light showed her thin yet curvy figure. They had taken a number of different pictures; some standing and some sitting, and one in a swimming suit, and then Masha and the agent had chosen the best ones and sent them off.

"She started getting letters right away," said Valentina, "And they kept coming. Masha wasn't that impressed with the quality of many of the letters, but some of the men were interesting. I would help her read them and write back to the men, and we used to have such a good time sitting in my kitchen, looking at her letters. We would put the photographs the men had sent in a row and weigh the pros and cons for each of them, trying to decide who Masha should write back to and which letters she should ignore."

Apparently, though, Masha had not mentioned in her Internet bio that she had a daughter, and each time she confessed this to a man to whom she was writing, he stopped writing back. But then Masha had started a very serious correspondence with a man in Norway. After a few months they had met in Moscow, applied for a visa at the Norwegian embassy there, and then, when her visa was issued, Masha moved to a small town in the northern part of Norway.

"She's married but she's still interested in the letters she's getting back here?" I asked, a little confused.

"She's not married, they're just living together," explained Valentina. "He said they would get married as soon as they were settled in Norway, but it hasn't happened yet. It's not as perfect as it sounds." Masha had discovered that her companion was drinking quite a bit. "And he doesn't have any friends of his own. So either they do things with his family or other Russian women. Masha is taking Norwegian lessons and has met other Russians in her class. Apparently there are other Russian women there, too, who have married Norwegian men." And, according to Valentina, Masha and her companion were arguing about money. Masha had not found work, but he still seemed to think that she should have her own money.

"*Nu, otkuda?* From where, though?" Valentina asked me rhetorically, "If she's not working . . ."

"What about her daughter?" I asked. "Is she planning to bring her daughter to Norway?" Valentina didn't say anything and just shrugged her shoulders.

"Does her companion know she has a daughter?"

"Yeah, I'm sure she's told him about Tanya," Valentina said, but it didn't sound as if she was sure. Reading between the lines I inferred that Masha had not mentioned her daughter, and was not planning to do so, either. But I also understood that Valentina did not want to talk about it.

"So, what about you?" I asked, to change the subject.

"I haven't gotten nearly as many letters as Masha," Valentina began. "But I have gotten some." She reached over and pulled the plastic bag of letters close to us. As she removed them from the bag she separated them into two piles, one of assorted sizes and envelopes, and one with identical, white, business-sized envelopes. She put the business envelopes to one side on the table and began shuffling through the first stack.

"Most of mine were from men who I didn't think were that interesting, either. And I got one from a man on death row, in Texas, which was kind of frightening." She laid a small envelope with her address printed on it in childlike letters on the table in front of me. "He said over and over that he was innocent, but I didn't write him back. Besides, he was black and Masha and I only wanted to write to white men." She put another, even smaller envelope on the top of the first. "And then I got this one."

I picked it up and pulled out a letter. When I unfolded the paper, a photograph of a short, overweight man slid out. He was completely naked.

It was not a very attractive picture and I set it on the table gingerly while grimacing at Valentina, who wrinkled her nose in agreement. The letter that went with the photograph was very short, too:

Dear Valentina,

I'm 43, sexy and a doctor. What do you like in Sex? Please send me sexy photographs of yours and return mine.

I love you,

Mario

I looked at the envelope again and noted that it was postmarked in Spain.

"I didn't answer him, either," Valentina said dryly.

"Do you get lots of letters from men in Europe?"

"I get some. Most of the women I know who are doing this are interested in men from either America or Germany, but I've gotten letters from all over: England, Egypt, Jordan. Right now I'm writing to a man from Canada, and I'm planning to go visit him in the fall."

"Exciting," I said, as she pulled out some photographs from another envelope and handed them to me. The first picture was of a man who looked about forty-five or fifty. He was also rather short and round, though wearing clothes, and he was standing in front of a small white house with another woman about his age. They were both covered in dirt and smiling for the camera.

"That's Wayne and his sister," said Valentina. She explained that she had been shocked when she first saw that photo. He had written in his letter that the picture was taken after they had spent the day digging potatoes at his sister's place. Valentina knew that he worked as a long distance truck driver, so he actually was employed, but to her the photograph spoke of poverty. Poverty and disrespect. I could understand why she had seen impoverishment. The photo did have a backwoods feel to it, and the work clothes the people were wearing had certainly seen better days, but then, they also looked like work clothes put on specifically for the task of digging potatoes. But Valentina, like most of her acquaintances, had probably survived through the years by supplementing her diet with homegrown potatoes. Actually, it was more likely that the food she managed to buy in the shops probably supplemented her diet of potatoes. To Valentina, digging potatoes was not an activity to be photographed and displayed for a potential mate; it spoke too clearly of an existence which was closer to subsistence than one would like to admit.

She told me again that she thought the photograph was disrespectful. "I sent him portraits taken at a professional studio, and he sent me a snapshot of himself with dirty fingernails!" She had felt this so strongly that she had written back to the man immediately and told him what she thought; if he wanted to impress her, he should send her a nice photograph, not one taken before he bothered to wash his hands.

Wayne understood. She showed me the next photograph he had sent her, a studio portrait of a clean and freshly shaved man in a pressed shirt.

"Then he sent me this one," continued Valentina, handing me another snapshot of the man at his computer. On the wall behind him were the two pictures Valentina had sent him, framed in dark wood and hanging next to each other. "He said that he'd bought a chair for me to sit in, if I should come to visit him, and he was sending me this picture, to prove it."

I looked again and saw that there was a pink armchair underneath the two photographs. I glanced up at Valentina, who said that she had felt a little bit uncomfortable when she had gotten that picture, thinking that maybe Wayne was moving too fast. But now she was thinking that she would probably give him a chance after all, and she had applied for a Canadian visa.

"Though you know, I wasn't that keen on him at first. I don't think he sounds very cultured. I know that truck drivers can be cultured, it isn't that, but I've tried to ask him about what books he likes or what type of music he listens to, and I get the feeling that he hasn't been exposed to very much classical literature or music. I don't expect him to have read Dostoyevsky or Pushkin, but I'd like my husband to at least enjoy the English classics." She paused and then continued. "I'm not sure he does. I've asked him which Shakespeare works he likes and he hasn't answered. Literature and music are things that I love, and I would like to be able to discuss them with my husband, to share that interest." She shrugged slightly. "I wrote that on my application, but I guess it's not really necessary."

She picked up the picture of Wayne at his computer. "He's living in a rented apartment. He said that he had a house once, but he lost it in his divorce. Do you think I should believe him? Does it work that way, that he could lose his home because of a divorce?"

I was unsure how to answer her, as I was unfamiliar with divorce laws in Canada. "I guess that could be the case," I said ambivalently. "It would sound reasonable."

She nodded, slightly reassured. "I'm going to go and visit him, but I feel a little more cautious now than I used to be." She pulled the stack of identical envelopes over to us and picked up the first one. "I'll tell you why. This is a very strange story," she began. "And why I decided to meet with you. I would like your opinion about this."

Showing me the first letter, she started to tell me about the relationship she called off six months ago. Sam had sent her his first letter about the same time as Wayne. She had written back to both of them, but it was obvious to Valentina that Sam was the better option, so, while she had continued to write to Wayne, her relationship with Sam became what she thought she had been searching for in all the other letters. He wrote two or three times a week, and his early letters were well written, poetic, and full of descriptions about his daily life. He shared with her his feelings, his political opinions, and his dreams.

"I tried to write the same type of letters back to him. I know my English wasn't that good, but he said it was fine, that he could understand my soul through my letters." They wrote to each other for a year and became more and more intimate in their correspondence. I looked at the stack of twenty or thirty letters and Valentina told me that they were only a small part of her collection from Sam.

"After we had been writing to each other for seven months, Sam asked me to marry him." I looked at her in surprise and she nodded her head yes. "But," she said, "I hesitated." She explained that there were some things about Sam which were not quite right, and she had become suspicious that he was not being completely honest with her.

Early on in their correspondence, Valentina had received an envelope from Sam which was addressed to her on the outside, but the letter inside was to a woman with a Chinese name. Valentina had confronted him about this immediately, and he had written a long and apologetic letter, in which he confessed that he had been having a relationship with a woman in China but promised her that he had ended it, that it was over now, and that Valentina was the only woman for him. He promised that he loved her, and only her.

She accepted the apology and didn't think much more about it until later, when other things started to awake her suspicions. For one thing, no matter how many times she requested more pictures of his life in the United States, he never sent any. The only photograph he mailed her during their entire correspondence was a little wallet-sized photograph. She showed me the picture of an overweight, bald man.

"I know he's not that physically attractive, objectively," she said, a little embarrassed. "But his words were so wonderful. I was really in love with him." However, as the letters he was writing to her became more and more intimate, they also became less well written. The grammar began to degenerate, and the language bordered on obscene. "I was really happy that we could have an adult relationship, even though we lived apart," said Valentina. "But sometimes I thought it was going too far."

What made her most suspicious, however, was that Sam refused to speak to her on the phone. She had sent him her telephone number and hinted that it would be nice to hear his voice, but he never rang. Calling abroad was very expensive for her, but after a while she decided that it would be worth it, just to feel a little closer to the man she had begun to fall in love with. So she wrote to Sam and asked him to send her his telephone number. At first he just ignored her request. She thought maybe her letter had gotten lost in the mail, or perhaps he had not understood how important it was to her, or had just forgotten. So she wrote again and asked him for his telephone number a second time.

Instead of sending his number, though, Sam wrote a long and complicated excuse about working undercover for the CIA. He said his missions were very dangerous and secretive, so the government changed his telephone number every twenty-four hours. He apologized for having lied to Valentina about what he did (he had told her first that he worked as a high school teacher) and asked her to just be patient, that eventually they would be able to speak. Then he said that he was thinking about trying to come and visit her.

The promise of a visit made Valentina really happy, even though she was surprised by, and a little suspicious about, his assertion that he was working for the CIA. It seemed hard to believe, especially given how rotund he appeared in his photograph. The CIA agents Valentina had seen in the movies were much more muscular. But that was Hollywood, and she wanted to believe Sam. After thinking about it for a while she wrote back with another suggestion.

"I told him he could send me the telephone number of a friend and then I could call him there. That's when I got this letter." She handed me another identical envelope. Like all the others, her address had been printed on a computer label and stuck on the outside, but Sam's return address sticker was missing. The letter inside was also written on a computer, like the rest of Sam's correspondence, but it was printed on plain paper, rather than the colorful, cloud-covered stationery of the other letters she had shown me. I started reading it and then looked at the signature at the bottom. It was from a woman who claimed to be Sam's mother. The letter said that Sam, her son, was very, very busy with his job, and that Valentina's pressure to give her a telephone number was making him unhappy. She asked Valentina to please stop nagging him about it and just believe that Sam loved her with all his heart, even though he could not talk to her in person.

I looked up at Valentina, who shook her head. "It was just all very strange," she said. "And he never wanted to take any concrete steps towards actually coming to visit, either. I mean, he asked me to marry him, but he wouldn't talk to me on the phone or come to meet me . . ."

The more Valentina thought about it, the more she became convinced that there was something wrong with their relationship, and with Sam. But it was a large step to go from being suspicious to actually ending the relationship. Finally, though, that is what she did.

"Ending it hurt a lot. I had grown to love Sam, or at least the Sam that I knew through his letters. I had spent my days dreaming about what our life was going to be like when we got married in America, and it was difficult to let go of those dreams. But I can deal with that hurt. That's all inside of me. And now I'm going to go visit Wayne in Canada, so I am moving on. What still bothers me, though, is not knowing if I did the right thing to

Sam. What if everything he told me was true, that he really did work for the CIA, that he was actually planning to come and visit, and that he really did want to marry me? What if he was being completely honest, if he really loved me, too, and my suspicions made me break the heart of a genuinely good man?"

Valentina's questions were not merely rhetorical; she was actually asking me what I thought. I looked at the pile of letters she had shown me. I broke tentatively from my interviewer role and started to shake my head. "He sounds dishonest," I said. And he did. The letter from his "mother" did not seem genuine to me, and neither did his story about the telephone numbers. "I don't think you made a mistake. Has Wayne called you on the phone?"

Valentina nodded. "Yes. He started calling me right away. Wayne is real. He seems a little simple, but I'm pretty sure I know what I'm getting with Wayne. Sam, on the other hand, seemed perfect. But I don't think perfect really exists. I think Sam was *too* good to be real." She handed me one of his envelopes again. "I've made up my mind to give Wayne a try, but I wanted to ask you to look at Sam's address and see if you thought it looked like he lives in a prison or a mental hospital."

I studied the address on the plain, white sticker, but it looked like a regular street address in a large American city. "If you let me copy it down in my notes, I can try to find out more about it when I get back," I said, and she nodded.

Valentina was done with what she wanted to tell me, so after writing down Sam's address I thanked her for taking the time to meet with me and share her story. We both stood up from the table and walked back out onto the square. Valentina walked a little ways with me before we came to the corner where she turned right and I went left.

"Thanks, again," I said to Valentina.

"I hope you find something out about Sam," she replied. Then she paused and took a breath. I stopped and waited for her to speak.

"You know," she said, "I've been doing this for six years now. When I first started, I thought it was going to be so easy. I would list the characteristics I wanted my husband to have, send off my photographs, and then the man who fit that description would write to me. I wasn't entirely naive. I mean, I wasn't expecting a prince, just someone who would be my companion and friend. But it hasn't worked like that at all. It's possible that Wayne is going to be someone I can live with, but I've come to realize that even with foreign men, I'm going to have to accept imperfections." She smiled and looked resigned. "But I want to find someone who understands me."

"I hope he's waiting for you in Canada," I said.

"I do too," she said, then turned and walked away.

{ 5 }

Tanya: Trafficking in Dreams

*J*ust before my research trip was over, I spent a couple of hours talking to Tanya. She was not one of the women I had written to. Rather, her older sister had asked me to meet with her. She and her family were concerned about Tanya's plans to move to America. They wanted me to make her reconsider, or at least try to warn her about what she was doing. According to her sister, twenty-one-year-old Tanya had recently sold her apartment to pay off some old debts and then used the rest of the money, $2,500 in U.S. dollars, to buy a visa and a ticket to America. She had done this through an agency which promised to have a man meet her at the airport in Los Angeles and help her find work. It sounded like the stereotypical trafficking set-up, and her family had been asking her not to go. But she was set on doing it.

Her family was right to be wary of the agency that Tanya was using to go to America. Stories abound in the former Soviet Union of women who are promised waitress or nanny jobs in the West but end up raped, beaten, stripped of their passports and identities, and "sold" to brothels in America, Europe, and the Middle East.[1] Trafficking of human beings is a huge and sordid business.[2] Young women answer ads for work abroad, or even become convinced by a boyfriend or a family member, in some cases, to take a chance on employment, only to find that once they leave their home country, they have been forced into the sex industry. Tanya's family was afraid this could happen to her, but she was ignoring their concerns.

I had no idea what I could say that would make a difference, especially given that, even if she'd had misgivings about going, it was not certain that Tanya could get out of the deal she had made with the "agency." If they were a trafficking ring, she would be worth too much money to be let off the hook, should she change her mind. In addition to the cash she was paying them, they would probably be able to get anywhere from three to ten thousand dollars for her when they sold her to a brothel. They would not let her back out, and the people running trafficking rings are known for resorting to extreme violence in order to control their victims. A life is not something they think twice about taking if a woman is not cooperating. Reports have appeared in the media of traffickers who shoot or even behead girls as an example in front of others they are trying to force into prostitution, as have stories of women who have been killed while escaping or upon returning home.[3] And one of the most effective tools traffickers have is to threaten not only the women but their families as well. Should she end up in America or elsewhere, Tanya would know that the people keeping her would have their contacts back in her hometown, ready to hurt her family and her child if she resisted their demands.

Going to the police in her situation would not have been a viable option, either. Nongovernmental organizations working with trafficked women report cases in the former Soviet Union where local police who are supposed to protect returned trafficked women have turned around and resold the women to the traffickers.[4] And even if Tanya's local police were not working in direct cooperation with the "agency" she was using, there is not much chance they would be either interested in or capable of protecting her.

Tanya had, however, agreed to meet me. I thought we could talk a little bit about her plans and what she expected to happen when she got to the States. She came over to the little apartment I was staying in, and we sat down in the kitchen to talk. Tanya had brought a large, leather purse with her and she sat up straight in one of the chairs with it on her lap. She, like Olga, was thin and beautiful, about five foot five, and dressed in trendy clothes like most of the women her age that I had seen in town. In contrast to Olga, though, Tanya's face looked hard and slightly cynical, and it was obvious from her body language that it was not her idea to come and talk with me. She agreed to drink some tea, though, and I found a match to light the stove with and put the teakettle on. While I waited for it to boil, I sat down at the kitchen table and tried to break the ice by explaining to Tanya what I was doing. I told her about my research and that I had been interviewing women who were writing to men in the West, that I was interested in the experiences these women had through their correspondence. She nodded and then she opened her purse.

"I brought some of the letters I've had from men, in case you want to see them." She took out a small bundle of letters and then clasped her purse shut again. "I don't have that many, but you can look at them if you want."

"I didn't realize that you've been writing to men," I said. "Ina told me that you were married."

"I am married," she said tiredly. "But about six months ago it became obvious that my marriage was ending, so I sent off my photo to the Internet. I didn't really know what to expect, but I thought I would give it a try."

I nodded. "Did you get anything interesting?"

Tanya shrugged wearily. The kettle boiled and I poured us both a cup of tea while she sifted through the letters.

"Almost right away I got this letter." She handed me a thick envelope and picked up her teacup while I opened it. "And it was curious, anyway." The stamp on the envelope was Canadian, but the postmark was illegible. Inside the envelope were six pages of cream-colored stationery with black and orange Celtic patterns in the margins. The pages were covered with words, typed in a single-spaced, nine-point font. Along with the letter was a strip of four photographs taken in one of those photo booths found in shopping malls.

"I think this guy is crazy," Tanya said. "Six pages and he only talks about himself. He says over and over again that he hates modernity. Apparently he lives in a cabin out in the woods somewhere, and he goes on and on about politics and about his dogs and hunting. I think he . . ." Tanya searched briefly for a word and then used the Russian phrase, "*suma soshel.*"

"He's lost his mind," I translated.

"Yes. He's lost his mind. And I think he is very interested in himself. I mean six pages! And in very small letters! And it's only at the very end of the letter that he writes a little bit about how he wants to get to know me and my son. But I don't even have a son. I have a daughter." Tanya let out an exasperated sigh. "This is the first letter I got, and it was from a *durak.*"

"Idiot." I gave her the word and she nodded.

"I didn't write back to him."

"I can understand why," I said.

"Anyway, he wasn't the only one who wrote to me. Altogether, in the last six months, I've gotten letters from nine men." She waited for my reaction and I raised my eyebrows slightly to indicate how impressive that was. She just shook her head, though. "Nine letters sounds like a lot, but they haven't really been the type of letters I was anticipating. Three of the men were already married. They were simply looking for entertainment."

I nodded and didn't mention that she herself was already married.

"Two of the men seemed to me to be sexually preoccupied. They only wrote about sex," she continued, selecting another letter from her stack and opening it. She turned to the back side of the letter and read, "I very much enjoy making love and it is important to me." Tanya looked at me and shrugged. "Making love is important to everybody," she said. "But I don't think you need to write that in the first letter you send to a stranger." Then she pulled out another letter and read, " 'Until then, my sweet, I will dream erotic and loving dreams of you in my arms . . .' Is that a normal way to end a letter in America?"

"Well, not really. Not for a first letter. But it sounds like he's trying to be romantic."

"Would you have answered a letter that ended like that?" she asked me.

"Nah," I shook my head slightly. "Probably not. It sounds a little cheesy."

"What do you mean by cheesy."

"It sounds a little exaggerated and false. The other three letters, though?" I asked her.

"Yeah, they were okay. They were from men who were seriously looking for a wife at least, and they sounded sort of normal." She put the letters about making love back into the stack and straightened it up by tapping all the letters lightly against the table. Then she laid them in her lap. "I've heard that American men want Russian wives because they want a housewife. Is that true?" Tanya looked straight at me and waited for an answer.

"That seems to be the impression I've gotten," I said, trying to be diplomatic. "Would that bother you?"

Tanya just snorted cynically. "That's what Russian men want, too. What's the difference?"

"Good point," I said, though Russian research indicates that Tanya, as a divorced woman, would statistically have a one in three chance of having been physically abused by her soon-to-be ex-husband,[5] as a corollary to her role as a domestic servant. Tanya may not have been abused, but it would not be out of the ordinary if she had. Some statistics suggest that 80 percent of violent crimes in Russia take place in the domestic sphere,[6] yet there seems to be political resistance against efforts to tackle abuse, and almost fifty different versions of a national law to address domestic violence have been shot down in parliament.[7] When it comes to police protection or legal prosecution of domestic violence in Russia, women's complaints are often met with responses like "she provoked it" or "it is a private affair."[8] The Russian Association of Crisis Centers for Women claims that 70 percent of the women calling their hotline have been refused help by the police,[9] and the attitude that the victim of domestic violence is to blame also influences the response women get from social workers and state-funded psychologists, many of whom aim to teach women how to avoid provoking an abusive husband rather than addressing the husband as the perpetrator of the problem.[10]

Those Russians working against this understanding of domestic violence are fighting an uphill battle. Larisa Babitskaya, a psychologist at a regional woman's shelter, notes that there is a favorite Russian adage which goes, "If he beats you, that means he loves you"; she points out that the first step in addressing domestic violence is to help the women realize that the saying is not true.[11] Babitskaya also says one change she has noted since the dissolution of the Soviet Union is that, as more women are staying home to take care of their family, those women suddenly realize that they have nothing to fall back on if their marriage turns sour. Even for women who do have jobs, divorce can be a difficult matter practically because of the lack of housing. Some women find they can be granted an official divorce but are still forced to live with their abusive partner. And stalking is barely even on the radar in terms of police protection. Tanya, at least, had managed to keep ownership of the apartment and made her husband move out, but it is possible she felt moving abroad was a good option because of the distance it would put between herself and her soon-to-be ex-husband. Presumably she would have a slightly better chance of avoiding both him and domestic abuse in the States. How much better American women have it can be debated, however. While it is probably easier to get the justice system to protect a woman in America, one in three American women will be physically assaulted by an intimate partner during her lifetime. And because of the rate of gun ownership, assault in the United States can be deadly. One-third of the women murdered in the United States are killed by their husbands.[12] Obviously, though, Tanya was willing to take her chances in America and the demand that she assume responsibility for domestic duties did not faze her.

"That's what all men want," she told me. "A friend of mine met an Italian man and moved there to live with him. He wants her to be at home and take care of their children, just like his mother did when he was young. But he also said that the choice to stay at home would be hers. If she really wanted to, she could work part time."

"Is she working now?" I asked.

"Not yet. She's still learning Italian. But she probably will. Anyways, if a person is going to be a housekeeper, it is better to do that somewhere else than here."

"Have you answered any of those letters?" I asked, nodding at the pile in her lap.

"Yes. I decided only to answer the ones I thought were interesting, so I didn't write to the men who seemed full of themselves, or crazy, or far too old. But I've written to a man from California." She selected another of the envelopes and took a photograph out of it. "Actually, I think he is a little too old, but I wrote to him anyway."

She handed me the photograph and I looked at a picture of a trim, gray-haired man standing next to the ocean.

"He's fifty. My perfect match would be someone who is maybe ten years older than me." She shrugged again and paused for a moment. Then she continued. "But he seems nice. And he doesn't mind that I already have a child, even though his children are already grown up. Actually, he already has a grandchild . . . He is older than I thought I would accept, but he has his own house and his own business, and he seems normal."

"He's thirty years older than you," I said.

"Yes. But none of the men who wrote to me were under forty. And maybe it doesn't make that much of a difference."

"Have you told him you're going to America?"

Tanya shook her head no. "But I might do that."

"What kind of work has this company said they will find for you?" I asked her.

"I'm just going to America to visit a friend," Tanya said and looked at me innocently.

"Oh. I thought you were going to work there."

"No, I'm just going to a friend's wedding." Then Tanya told me a completely different version of her plans than what I had heard from her sister. According to Tanya, she was going to LA because a friend of hers was getting married. Her friend had originally planned to move to California to marry a man she'd been writing to, but a couple of weeks before she was going to leave, the man had called everything off. It sounded like he had just gotten cold feet and decided he didn't want to go through with things. He stopped calling her at the agreed upon times, he didn't send any more letters, and when she had tried to call him on the telephone, he hung up as soon as he realized who it was. Tanya's friend had been heartbroken, but after thinking it through she had decided to go to America anyway. She had a ticket and a visa, and she knew someone who had emigrated to LA a few years earlier. So she got on the plane to the United States and has been living there ever since.

"At first she really hated it," said Tanya. "She used to cry every time she called me and she really missed the Russian language." But she found work doing home care for the elderly, she learned how to understand and speak American English, and she made friends. And then she listed herself with a dating agency in LA. "She was popular because she was Russian," said Tanya. Her friend started dating, and fairly quickly she found a lawyer who was interested in her. He proposed and it was their wedding that Tanya was planning to attend.

Tanya said she intended to be gone for only three months, primarily because she was not sure that she would like American culture and she wanted to give it a try before deciding to move there more permanently. She was planning to bring four hundred dollars with her, and her friend had promised to help her find work as a waitress once she was there, to support herself. She said she would be leaving her daughter here, with her mother, but that if she decided she liked America she would definitely bring her daughter there to live with her. Then she started quizzing me about life in the United States.

"How much does food cost in Hollywood?" she asked me.

"LA is expensive," I said. "Four hundred dollars isn't going to last you three months. You'll definitely need to get a job."

"My friend says it won't be a problem to find a job as a waitress."

"Maybe not," I said. "You can look in the newspaper, too. And restaurants sometimes put help wanted signs up in their windows."

Tanya asked me if she could travel anywhere she wanted to in America on a tourist visa. I assured her she could, and that once she was in the country no one would check her passport. Then she asked if it was true that American women pay for their share of the bill at a restaurant.

"Yeah, sometimes. It's not uncommon," I said.

"How do I say 'to each pay half' at a restaurant?" she asked me.

"Let's split it."

"Let's split it," Tanya tested out the phrase. "Is it true that American men are afraid of American women? Are American women really all feminists?"

I cringed underneath my neutral interviewing smile and realized we were back to the issue of feminists again. I thought about the danger of being trafficked that Tanya was facing and felt like telling her she had a lot more to be frightened of than American feminists. But I knew that message would not get through. From my Western viewpoint, the need for a feminist movement in Russia is glaring, not least because issues like prostitution, domestic abuse, inadequate reproductive care, sexual harassment, and unequal pay are rarely addressed in mainstream politics.[13] But Tanya would probably not agree. Issues that American feminists, for example, may think are important are not necessarily issues that Russian women's groups would want to address. Some of these differences may stem from experiences with the state and the public and private spheres. Basu notes, for example, that women's groups in former communist nations seem to be more concerned with issues that address employment, political representation, and welfare whereas in countries which have a political history of liberal democracies, issues that deal with the private sphere like domestic violence, women's health, and reproductive rights are more often addressed by women's groups.[14] This difference in focus can explain in part why Russian women's organizations sometimes criticize international funding bodies for emphasizing projects that address foreign concerns rather than listening to what Russian activists think are particularly important issues.[15] Russian women, the American men writing to them, and Russian women's groups are not alone in critiquing Western feminism; outside North America and Europe, feminism is often associated with Western imperialism and neocolonialist politics, economic "development," and modernization.[16] Within academic circles, the concept of a global feminist movement has also come under fire,[17] especially because of the way it can patronize and belittle women in non-Western countries, assuming that they need to be saved from their local patriarchal structures. Global feminism is also accused of ignoring the diversity within the category "woman." Women are oppressed and empowered differently within and across nations and these important differences can be lost when a global feminist discourse assumes a universal oppression of women.[18] This means that the social action to change the problems Tanya was facing in her community would have to be a very Russian movement, one that politically and theoretically addresses the historical conditions pertaining to women in the former Soviet Union rather than being a copy of Western versions of feminism.[19] And to be successful, it would probably have to masquerade under a different name.

When I later spoke with Tanya's sister and told her what Tanya had said her plans were, she was convinced that Tanya had been lying. "I know she's already paid someone to take her abroad and find her work," her sister said. "She's probably trying out her INS story on you to see if it's believable." And that may be true. There were things about Tanya's story which I found difficult to believe, above all that she, a young, soon-to-be single Russian woman of limited means, would have been granted a tourist visa to the United States through regular channels. And the fact that she had sold her apartment also suggested she was planning to do more than visit.

Tanya, however, was a very bright and motivated young woman, and she obviously had her reasons for doing what she was doing. One of the things traffickers rely on is the ignorance and naiveté of their victims, but there are more and more reports in the Russian and Eastern European media about trafficking, and charitable organizations are working along with some governmental authorities to disseminate information to young girls and their families and heighten awareness about the dangers.[20] Obviously Tanya and those close to her had heard these reports and were aware and concerned for her sake. But there must have been other issues that would make her willing to risk the danger of being trafficked into prostitution. It has been suggested that some women paying "employment agencies" to take them out of Russia may be aware that they can end up working as sex workers, at least for a while, but think that this is an acceptable alternative to staying where they are (and perhaps having to do the same thing in Russia), at least for a time.[21]

This reality became obvious to me halfway through the year I was studying in Russia. I had just spent another day listening to lectures in my winter coat and fur hat, along with all the other students. Rumors were circulating that earlier in the fall the city's mayor had sold all the municipal heating fuel for cash and then moved abroad. Since the city's infrastructure was built up on the concept of district heating, all the buildings—the library, the university, the hospitals, and apartment buildings—were heated from central stations that pumped steam into radiators around town. And since there was not much fuel to make steam with, there was not much heat in any of the buildings. Thankfully one of the Nordic countries had donated a little fuel to the city when news of the fraud came out, and buildings were being kept just above the freezing point, but winters in Russia are cold and on that day in February I felt as if I had been frozen for five months. So when I walked out into the gray dusk of late afternoon and realized it was snowing again, I just sighed. But then I caught sight of one of the other American exchange students, waved, and was overwhelmed by a homesick longing to go and grab a hamburger and beer in a warm college bar.

Our chances of finding a college bar or a decent hamburger were nonexistent, but beer was one thing the town had plenty of. Josh suggested we meet at the bar in the largest hotel later, and I managed to contact two other Americans in town. When we gathered that evening it turned out that the bar even had an electric heater. It was warm enough to sit without our coats on, and we were speaking English the whole evening.

It felt decadent. The first round of beers went down quickly and it almost felt like home. We sat and discussed how the last couple of weeks had been, the classes we were taking, what new Russian words we had learned recently, the respective qualities of Russian and Estonian beer, and the various stages of culture shock.

When it was my turn to buy the next round, I managed to convince everyone to try Lapin Kulta, the Finnish beer that was a new import in all the kiosks. I went and stood at the bar, waiting to get the attention of the bartender. Suddenly I realized that the middle-aged man in a gray suit next to me had put his arm around my waist. I turned and looked at him, and he slurred out in a very thick Finnish accent, "Upstairs, yes? Us!"

I leaned back and tried to fan away the cigarette and alcohol smell from his breath. "What?" I asked, first in Russian.

"No. No Russian. English. You, how much?"

"What?" I said, this time in English.

"My hotel room, upstairs. Come on."

"I am *not* a prostitute. Get your hands off me," I said, and turned back to the bar.

"How much?" he said again, obviously not understanding and trying to put his arm back around my waist. Thankfully, Josh had seen what was going on and managed to diplomatically slide in between me and the man while also attracting the attention of the bartender. Together we brought the drinks back to our table.

"Jeez," I said and told the others what the guy had suggested.

"Yeah, but look who he got instead," said Ann, who was in some of my classes.

I looked back at the bar again and saw that the Finn was picking up one of the Russian girls who was a member of our history of philosophy class.

"I think that both she and Nadezhda are working here," Ann continued, nodding toward the other end of the bar where another of our classmates was being courted by a *beezneez* man. Neither of the girls indicated in any way that they had noticed us, and we didn't approach them, either. What they were doing was not our business, and all of us were aware that the student stipends were hard to stretch. I knew we were all feeling uncomfortable in the face of such blatant injustice: that we as exchange students could eat—when there was food to buy—because we had dollars, while our classmates who didn't had to find other ways to secure their daily bread. Employment options for female students were very limited, and limited for young women in general. This may suggest what some of the women who end up trafficked are thinking. If prostitution is the option a young woman has at home, doing the same thing abroad might not seem so unthinkable.

This is an important consideration because it is an explanation that grants a semblance of agency to the women who are being trafficked out of the former Soviet Union, something that is otherwise easy to lose sight of in literature about trafficking. All too often trafficked women are presented as passive, helpless victims of the mafia and the criminal underworld populating the sex industry, but they are often very ambitious and risk-taking individuals. That said, of course, once entrapped the women are harnessed through "debt" to their pimps and enslaved to brothels or individuals from whom they can't escape,[22] and their agency quickly slips away.

According to the UN protocol dealing with trafficking in humans,[23] trafficking is "the recruitment, transportation, transfer, harboring or receipt of persons, by means of the threat or use of force or other forms of coercion, of abduction, of fraud, of deception, of the abuse of power or of a position of vulnerability . . . or of the giving or receiving of payments or benefits to achieve the consent of a person having control over another person, for the purpose of exploitation."[24] There is nothing in this definition which limits trafficking to the sex industry, or its "victims" to the female gender. While discussions of trafficking tend to focus on issues of prostitution and the sexual exploitation of women, humans are trafficked across borders for other reasons as well, including agricultural and sweatshop labor, the illegal adoption of children, forced marriages, organ transplants, drug trafficking, and begging.[25] Many of the same issues which work as push and pull factors for the women are just as applicable to men and children. Even though it makes for less dramatic news coverage, men are also trafficked. However, except for the case of adoption, young women are often seen as the most desirable commodity, even outside the sex industry. They are in demand because they are thought to be more compliant and submissive, less likely to rebel or try to escape, and more detail-oriented. The majority of trafficked people are women and girls; the International Organization for Migration estimates that each year between 700,000 and two million women and children are trafficked across international borders,[26] by traditional trafficking rings and by maid schemes, as domestic servants, and by mail-order bride companies.[27] The root causes of this are unequal gender relations and patriarchic value systems which discriminate against women and girls and facilitate violence, sexual abuse, and their exploitation, in both the sending and receiving communities, in the household, the family, and the public arena.[28] Because discrimination is at the bottom of the value systems that allow and encourage trafficking, attempts to stop it must focus on not only material poverty but also the poverty of rights and entitlements. Addressing trafficking has to entail empowering women.[29]

Tanya, like many women, must have had her reasons for initially making contact with the people promising to help her move to the United States, reasons which probably did not differ significantly from any of the "push factors" that encourage other women (and men) to take the risk-filled step of using shady or illegal means for moving abroad. The collapse of local governing structures and the socialist systems in the countries of the former Soviet Union and China, and the increase of civil war and ethnic conflicts in these regions, act as contributing factors, as do environmental damage, natural disasters, domestic violence, uneven economic growth, and general economic decline.[30] These factors sometimes hit women disproportionately hard, especially when their unequal rights limit their life choices and opportunities for formal employment. The fact that the women I interviewed repeatedly mentioned their dismay at not being able to find appropriate work with dependable pay is an example of how poverty is gendered, which, when combined with a high frequency of sexual harassment in the workplace and violence against women in both the public and the private spheres, is a push factor that influences their desire to move abroad.[31]

Having a reason to leave and search for opportunities somewhere else works in conjunction with the fact that globalization has increased the freedom of movement for capital, goods, and individuals from wealthier countries, while immigration laws in many Western nations have become increasingly stringent and restrictive to keep out asylum seekers and economic migrants.[32] Push factors like corruption and the breakdown of law and order in their home countries, combined with a restrictive international legal migration framework, increase the chance that women will fall victim to traffickers; trafficking can be their only chance when feasible legal migration options are so limited.[33]

There are also pull factors that contribute to trafficking. While Western governments have become more restrictive of the numbers and types of legal migrants allowed into their boarders, the labor markets in these countries are, at the same time, becoming more dependent on migrant labor.[34] A need for cheap immigrant labor and government restrictions on migration are not the apparent contradiction they would first seem. Illegal labor is less expensive and less likely to complain than individuals who are legally allowed to live and work in a country, so restrictive immigration policies provide industry with a low-paid and submissive workforce that does not demand the social benefits a legal citizen can command.[35] Trafficked humans can end up in precarious labor situations, bonded to a sweatshop or "employed" for rates of pay far below the official wage, with little or no redress because of their illegal status. This situation is starting to change in the United States, as labor unions have begun to enfranchise illegal laborers rather than agitating against their employment, but current public debate about immigration still tends to build on anti-immigrant rhetoric about stolen jobs.[36] On the larger scale, addressing the trafficking of humans means addressing the political and economic structures which restrict the legal movement of labor from developing countries and allow for the exploitation of illegal labor.[37]

The trafficking of laborers tends only to make the news when a disaster happens: when fourteen Mexicans died from heat and dehydration in the stretch of Arizona desert that they had to cross to meet their traffickers;[38] and when nineteen Chinese laborers drowned picking cockles off England's coast as the tide waters came in too quickly;[39] when fifty-eight Chinese men and women suffocated as they were smuggled across the English Channel into the UK on a produce truck.[40] Or, occasionally the media will direct attention to the "waves" of "asylum seekers" attempting to cross the Mediterranean into Europe on substandard boats who end up adrift, first in the water and then in a bureaucratic network of asylum policies.[41]

These workers may not have been moved across a border against their will, but they can be considered trafficked and exploited. And like Tanya, they probably made active decisions about migrating. In the case of women who are trafficked into prostitution, conflicting understandings of what women do and why, whether they know what awaits them at the other end of their journey or whether they are ensnared into forced prostitution, is an ambiguity reflected in the division that exists between organizations contending with trafficking. There are different ideas about where to draw the line between trafficking and migration, and of how or if to make a distinction between free and forced prostitution.[42] The distinction between illegal immigrants and trafficked humans, whom to deport and whom to assist, is hotly contested between governments and nongovernmental organizations. Unfortunately, governments tend to conflate trafficking with undocumented migration, the results of which mean the victims of traffickers are prosecuted or deported while the traffickers escape. This situation also illustrates the fact that many countries have a two-tiered human rights approach, reserving human rights and access to the justice system for citizens and denying these to noncitizens, something that is not supported by international human rights law but is enacted in practice.[43]

Those services which are available to victims of trafficking in their host countries have tended to focus on the moment of "rescue" from prostitution and the consequences immediately thereafter. In the United States and many European countries, victims are forced to choose between cooperating with the police in prosecuting their traffickers and thereby gaining a temporary right to remain in the country and, sometimes, access to social services, or being deported immediately.[44] And in some countries, trafficked women rescued from brothels are forced into "rehabilitation" programs and remand homes in which they meet abuse and exploitation from those who are supposed to help them, raising the question of how assistance can be provided in a way which does not mimic the controlled existence in which their traffickers were keeping the women originally.[45]

Formal, legal protection of trafficked women has been criticized for forcing the cooperation of victims while potentially exposing them, and their families back in their home countries, to the danger of reprisals. It has also been criticized for offering only short term support for victims.[46] Compounding this problem is the fact that many trafficked people are distrustful and fearful of the police and other governmental organizations. Their illegal-migrant status can be used against them, and they can be sent home after their traffickers have been brought to trial or in the mass deportations that sometimes occur after brothel raids in Europe.[47] Because of the distrust trafficked women can feel for officials, human rights and women's organizations are important alternative actors in both providing help and assistance and in raising general awareness and lobbying for change.[48] When it comes to helping victims of trafficking, NGOs can provide different levels of support than the state can, everything from telephone advice to housing, vocational training, return and reintegration services, and psychological support.[49] And at every level that support is dearly needed.

However, while nongovernmental assistance for victims of trafficking is necessary, especially when the state will not or cannot assist them, there has been criticism of the help provided to victims. It has been asserted that behind the services available from NGOs lurks an image of trafficked women as passive victims. Viewing the women as vulnerable objects in need of being rescued and rehabilitated ignores a different reality; women who have fallen victim to traffickers are often driven individuals like Tanya who have made a rational decision to migrate based on compelling reasons that still exist even once they are "rescued." Being freed from their traffickers does not mean their life situation in their home country has changed.[50]

But how are trafficking victims related to mail-order brides? This is the same question Vera's interview forced on me. Often they are grouped together in discussions of trafficking, yet there are significant differences in their experiences and status. Trafficked women receive help after they have been "rescued" by the police, discovered in passport checks, or if they manage to escape by themselves or with the help of clients,[51] and generally those trafficked women who are offered assistance are somehow related to the sex industry. For foreign fiancées and wives who have been imported only to find themselves abused by their husbands, there is often less protection, and just as much fear of deportation. Thankfully, this is slowly changing, and the United States now allows an immigrant woman to file a visa petition on her own if her husband is abusive,[52] but there is still more to be done. The International Human Rights Law Group suggests that there should be in place a system which informs fiancées about their legal rights in the destination country and puts them in contact with local NGOs to which they can turn in case of need. They also make the point that women should be presented with official government reports detailing their future husband's financial situation, criminal background, current and previous marriages, and, in particular, previous marriages to immigrant women.[53] Lawmakers in the United States are beginning to take this issue seriously, particularly after a number of high profile cases in which mail-order brides have been abused and even murdered by their husbands.[54] The International Marriage Broker Regulation Act has begun to regulate the visa application process more justly, including mandatory criminal background checks on the men which are disseminated to their potential fiancées.[55]

However, there is some debate about putting mail-order brides and women who are trafficked into forced prostitution into the same category. There are reports, of course, that some traffickers recruit victims with offers of marriage, and that "international marriage brokers" are used to facilitate trafficking, even of minors.[56] Thinking back to the shopping cart Web icons on the mail-order bride site I had initially used to buy the women's addresses, there was an undeniable aspect of commercialism involved that turned the women into objects to be bought and sold. Mail-order brides do share some of the same push and pull factors as other trafficked individuals. They are responding to the dream of a better life, and it would seem that they are often being imported because of their reputation for subservience. One of the more outspoken agencies tackling the mail-order bride phenomenon in America is the Coalition Against Trafficking in Women. Its co-executive director, Dorchen Leidholdt, warns that abuse in mail-order bride marriages is predictable, especially because the agencies market the women as submissive and docile,[57] traits which appeal to men who have issues with control. Leidholdt also makes the point that Russian women may not always be getting the family-oriented husbands they think they are trading-up for.[58] On the other hand, except for Tanya, I did not get the impression that the women I met were paying traffickers or at risk of being sold through rings of criminal gangs. They seemed to be tackling the details of migration together with their future partner. And for the women I met, the dream of being a wife and a mother was at least as influential as the dream of a better material existence in their search for a husband. I have no doubt some of them could end up in abusive relationships, but I wondered if they could really be considered victims of trafficking.

But then, as I was researching the issue of trafficking more closely after having conducted the interviews, I came across a report compiled from information provided by Norwegian women's shelters. The report presented statistics on an increasing number of foreign women who were seeking shelter from abusive men who had imported three and four foreign wives in a row, and who were being subjected not only to servitude and violence in the home but also forced to sexually service the men's friends and, in some cases, prostitute themselves in order to "earn their keep."[59] The report made me think again of Valentina's friend Masha, in Norway with a fiancé and obviously still interested in potential suitors sending her letters back home. I wondered what her life was really like in Norway. Some of the stories of immigrant wives abused in the United States mirror the situation in Norway. At the same time, there are cases of couples who have legitimately met through the Internet, who have overcome or accepted the power differences that exist between a Western husband and an imported fiancée, and who are happy in their relationships. Mail-order brides can end up in terrible situations. But the phenomenon can also lead to a relationship that satisfies both partners' desires and looks like a normal middle-class marriage—whatever that may be. There is a whole spectrum of possible outcomes.

Regardless of whether or not a bride is trafficked, though, the fact remains that, like all individuals in a community, she ought to be entitled to protection of her human rights by the law and by those around her. Regardless of whether Masha had agreed to move in with her fiancé in Norway or was being kept against her will, she ought to be entitled to the same protection as any other woman in her town. I hoped that Masha would be able to come in contact with Norwegian organizations willing to help her if she found herself in a compromising or dangerous situation. And for those women who end up in America, it is important to underline the necessity of the International Marriage Broker Regulation Act, which can possibly help women avoid abusive relationships and make their situation as mail-order brides a little less precarious.

But that proposed legislation did not help me there in the interview, when I was trying to figure out what to say to Tanya. After talking a little bit about feminism in the United States and trying to explain to her that not all American men were afraid of all American women, I tried to warn her about the dangers that could be awaiting her in the United States. I felt that I had to respect the version of her plans that she had given me, but I still told her that it did happen that young Russian women were sometimes trafficked into prostitution, and that in the United States at least she would be able to go to the police and they would help her even if she was not a citizen. I explained to her how to call the emergency services, and that she would not be automatically deported if she contacted them. And I told her that it might be a good idea to write to the man in California and tell him about her plans to be in the United States, just so someone there would be waiting to see her and would be concerned if she failed to show up.

"Yeah," she said, nodding at my advice. "But my friend is there, too." She stood up and I followed her to the doorway. "It's been nice to meet you," she said.

"You, too," I concurred. "Thank you. And good luck." Once again I stopped myself from stretching out my hand just in time. Tanya put her purse over her shoulder, returned my smile, and left. I went back to the kitchen to wash the teacups and hoped she would be okay.

6

Marina: Culture Shock

*A*fter I finished my Russian interviews, I headed back to the university and wrote up my report. But even after the research project was done, I kept thinking about the women I had met. I kept wondering how things were for those women who managed to find a man. I wondered if they really found their "love and future happiness." I wondered how they dealt with the culture shock that met them. And I wondered if they found all those scary feminists they had been warned about. So a few years later, I spoke with Russian brides in America. Their stories about real life after moving to the United States were just as illuminating as the dreams that women in the former Soviet Union had told me, but they all touched upon the cultural adjustment that met them. Some of the women used the term "culture shock," some of them spoke only of differences between the countries, but all of them talked about the practical details of learning to live in America and learning to live with a new partner.

Two of the women I interviewed in the United States had brought their children with them, and they emphasized that the process of adapting to the new country was one the entire family had to go through. That involvement also extended beyond the nuclear family. In a startling parallel to my interview with Olga and her mother, I spoke with one woman, Marina, whose American mother-in-law had been instrumental in initiating and facilitating her son's search for a bride. When I interviewed her mother-in-law, she gave me her own perspective on the process of finding a bride for her son and then trying to help the Russian bride make the adjustments to America. I include her version of the process to counter the stereotype of Russian brides who find themselves isolated and cloistered by lonely, possessive men. This is undoubtedly the situation for some women, and not just mail-order brides. Research on women who enter into arranged marriages and migrate from South Asia to the UK, United States, or Canada, for example, has also shown that these women some-times find themselves isolated and with little access to familial support, despite what are perhaps more intricate immigrant support networks than those which the Russian women can access.[1] But for some of the Russian women I met, they were not only entering into new relationships with their husbands; they were also moving into new networks of families and friends, with social ties that need to be established, negotiated, and main-tained even through the period of culture shock and adjustment.

Marina's mother-in-law lived about ten miles away from her son and Marina and had her own job and busy life, so she was not as focused on helping them with the day-to-day practicalities of running their house-hold as a Russian *babushka* would have been. But the similarities between their relationship in America and that of Olga and her mother back in the former Soviet Union were uncanny. I remembered how, when I was drinking tea at Olga's place, it had struck me that the close bond she and her mother shared would make it difficult for a man to enter into her life. Olga and Anya's bond was largely built on the mother-daughter relation-ship, but also on the fact that they were both women and could share experiences a man would never understand. Marina and her American mother-in-law were not as close as Olga and Anya, and they did not interact in the eerily symbiotic way that Olga and Anya had, but there was still a strong relationship developing between them when we spoke.

When I asked Wendy to explain the part she had played in bringing Marina and Robert together, she told me that a couple of years back her son had decided to give up his search for a woman to marry. He had announced this over one of those stereotypical Sunday dinners when the mother asks her grown-up son when he is going to find a wife. In exas-peration he had said that he was not going to. Like many of the other men who write testimonials on the mail-order bride websites, or who have spoken to the press about Russian brides,[2] or who have expressed their feelings in the letters the women showed me, Robert had said that he was tired of American women who thought they were better than him and were only focused on their career, not on him. He said that what he wanted to find was an old-fashioned girl, one who cooked and took care of him, and one who was nice and loyal. Wendy's reaction, when she heard this, was to try to find a mail-order bride for her son on her own. She admitted that her friends all thought she was crazy, but she figured she knew her son better than anyone else did, so she was in the best position to find him a suitable wife.

Later that week, after his announcement, Wendy went on the Internet and did a search for mail-order brides, and that was when she found many of the Russian mail-order bride sites, sites which assured their readers that Russian women were not going to compete with their American husbands. As one of the companies selling addresses says, a Russian woman "expects to be treated as a lady, she is the weaker gender and knows it. The Russian woman has not been exposed to the world of rampant feminism that asserts its rights in America." Sometimes this rhetoric can be cloying, as, for example, in this observation: "Her eyes can speak of the trials and hardship of a struggling country, but they can laugh with the indomitable spirit of mother Russia. Imagine if they laughed with you and gave you all they had!"[3] The image of Russian women that is being sold obviously appeals to a lot of men, since the industry is huge and seems to be growing. The assurances of a noncompetitive bride appealed to Wendy, too.

While she was surfing, Wendy also found a site with information about the scams a person can run into when writing to Russian mail-order brides.[4] She read the warnings carefully so she could avoid getting caught in them, warnings that resonated with simple commonsense advice, such as not sending money to a woman one has never met, not even if it is allegedly for the purpose of buying her a ticket to come and meet the man. These warnings attempt to convince the men to be realistic in their searches for a woman, suggesting that women who are fifteen to twenty years younger than they are, and are beautiful, may have hidden agendas, though Olga's and Tanya's experiences would suggest that many men disregard that advice. But the sites repeatedly caution men to avoid "gold diggers." The warnings also include cautions about women who are eager to convey their deep and intimate feelings to a man very quickly; as one site says, "Russian ladies have huge problems expressing their feelings in general, and even more problems with English."[5] A woman who is very good at this may be good at it because she has had a lot of practice. Likewise, these sites claim that most Russian women who do have access to the Internet only check their e-mail once a week, at best, so a woman who writes back right away may generate a suspicion that she is a gold digger.[6] Most mail-order-bride sites give some sort of advice on how to avoid being had and then leave the rest up to their clients. But a few of the companies even claim to have policies designed to check on the women to make sure they are acting honestly. How well this can work in an industry that is largely based on the anonymity of the Internet can be debated. But many of the smaller, local agencies in Russia have personal contact with their female clients. Vera, for example, dealt with each woman herself. And even the purely virtual companies can do random spot checks of the e-mail services they provide and remove the listings of women they suspect of committing fraud.[7] But sometimes "fraud" is not necessarily the women's fault. One of the women I met in America said that in her town the women had been using a photographer who promised them pictures that were good for the Internet. He had taken decent photographs and offered very reasonable rates, but after a while many of the women started being blacklisted from sites they did not even know they were on. It took some time, but finally it came out the photographer had been selling copies of their pictures to other agencies without the women's permission, spreading their images around with false identities.

So Wendy read up on what to avoid before starting her search, and when she felt she knew enough not to be deceived and was ready to find her son the perfect Russian wife, she started choosing the girls to whom to write. She read through the listings of women carefully, paying attention to their personal descriptions and the type of men they were looking for, and then she began picking out possible candidates whom she thought would be appropriate for her son. She chose twenty women who seemed to fit her criteria, ordered their addresses, and sat down to write to them, pretending to be her son. Then she waited. It was only a couple of weeks before the letters started arriving. Each day she would walk down to the end of her driveway around noon, after the mailman had come, and sift through the bills and junk mail to find the letters with Russian stamps addressed to her son. When most of the replies had arrived, she and her son went through the letters together and chose four women to respond to. And eventually, after a bit more correspondence, they narrowed it down to one: Marina.

When they had chosen Marina, Wendy felt obligated to write to the other women and tell them that it was actually she who had been involved in the initial correspondence. She was a little uneasy about how they would react to this, especially since all her friends in America had been so wary of what she was doing. But Wendy said that none of the women in Russia seemed to think her actions were odd or out of place. According to Wendy, mothers in Russia are much more active in finding a partner for their sons than in America and the women she had written to thought what she was doing was not so unusual. "They had the same thoughts I did," she told me. "They knew that I'm the one who knows my son best." I thought that Olga and Anya would agree.

Once they had decided on Marina, Robert got a tourist visa and flew to the provincial capital of the region Marina lived in. Marina met him at the airport. Wendy's voice took on a romantic tone when she told me about their meeting. Robert had brought a diamond ring with him and he proposed to Marina right there in the airport. Then, after spending a day in the capital, they took an eight-hour train ride through the fields and forests to the small industrial city where Marina lived.[8] When the train pulled to a stop in front of the run-down station and Robert and Marina stepped down onto the single platform, Robert found himself embraced in a bear hug, being greeted warmly and very physically by Marina's father. "Robert was a little shocked by the hug," Wendy told me. But he went along with that tradition and all the others the two of them had to uphold in connection with their engagement.

Marina could speak English, but except for one cousin who had studied at a private school, the rest of her family could speak only Russian. So Marina became Robert's translator during most of the visit. This worked well, and it also meant that certain moments became even more intimate for the two of them because they had to be shared. For example, when Robert asked Marina's father for her hand in marriage, Marina had to be there to translate, and she got tears in her eyes. Marina's father spelled out his conditions for allowing Robert to marry her: he wanted to know how Robert would make sure Marina was okay even if something happened to him; and that Robert would see to it that she could continue her studies in America if she wanted to. Robert assured him that Marina would be taken care of, and that his parents in the United States would be there for her if something should happen to him. And he also assured him that she could keep studying at the university. When Marina had translated these promises back into Russian, she was quickly able to translate back to Robert that their marriage met his approval.

Because they were engaged, it was acceptable, and expected, that they would need some privacy to get to know each other better, so Marina's parents temporarily moved out of the flat they shared with Marina and into the grandmother's place. And the family also threw a big engagement party for them, with hot meat patties and chicken, cold cuts and rye bread, beet salads and pickles, potatoes in many different forms, and lots and lots of vodka. Russian weddings are big events, lasting for two or three days and involving friends and family by the dozens, lots of songs and practical jokes, and many, many toasts to the newlyweds. But because Robert and Marina were going to get married in the States, their engagement party took on a more festive mood than it may normally have done—both more festive and more serious. At the party, and in front of all the guests, Marina's father gave them his blessing. He took their hands in his, held them firmly, and wished them happiness and good fortune in the future. Then Marina's mother did the same thing, wishing them a happy, loving home. The next day Marina's grandmother blessed them, asking God to watch over both them and their future children. Even through the translating, Robert understood how earnest their words were, and no one's eyes were dry when the blessings were done.

Robert stayed with Marina and her family for two weeks, getting to know her and taking the all important photographs of their time together to show the embassy as part of her visa application. He was also learning about the culture she came from, and the differences in their life experiences, knowledge that would obviously be useful when they were back in America and he would need to explain to her many of the daily things most people take for granted.

After he left, Marina applied for what is colloquially called a fiancée visa, which allows the woman to live in the United States for ninety days to get to know her future husband better. During that time she has to get married to an American or leave the country at the end of those ninety days. With this visa, once the woman is married, she can submit her application for a green card.[9] Marina and Robert got married within a month of her arrival, like many couples who do not wait the full ninety days before tying the knot. Many couples live together for a couple of weeks to test things out and then get married and apply for the green card. And for all the women I came in contact with, the process of getting a green card took much longer than expected. This means that, once their fiancée visa expires and before the green card comes through, the women are in a legal gray zone, most for over a year. This can make it difficult for them to apply for a driver's license, for example, or travel abroad. But it is not just their legal status that is uncertain for the women during their first year in America. The culture shock they encounter can be just as disconcerting. Especially the first few weeks of the woman's stay seem to involve many initial adjustments, both for the man, who suddenly finds himself living with another person, and most of all for the woman, who has to make an adjustment to an entirely different culture as well as get used to a new relationship.

The industry is aware of this, and some of the larger sites provide online tips for the men on how to get through these first few weeks. It is also one of the main topics covered in discussion groups and testimonial sites about marrying Russian women.[10] The subjects center on "what your lady will need" and how the man can prepare for her arrival, now that he has found the "perfect jewel from the Former Soviet Union."[11] Some of the most interesting suggestions point to culture clashes that tend to characterize Russian-American marriages, everything from the way women dress to what they eat.

First and foremost, it appears as if adjusting to American food can be difficult for the women, and the men are warned about this. One site recommends that the men find Russian grocery stores nearby, something most urban areas now have, or consider buying Russian foods through the Internet. It is recommended that they do this right away when their wife arrives, in order to help her adjust.[12] When it comes to American food, the men are warned to avoid spicy foods (Mexican and Cajun food in particular appear to cause problems) and to stick to fruits, vegetables, and other "bland" foods until they figure out what their lady likes. The men are warned that their bride is probably not going to like American bread, but that beets, onions, cucumbers, and radishes should go down well. Ice cubes and cold drinks will probably be exotic for the women, and tea is always good to have around. And as much as this advice seems to take on the same sort of tone as an article on "what to feed your new puppy," the suggestions do appear to reflect what the women I met experienced.

According to the discourse on these sites, introducing the women to America and showing them around their new home also involves familiarizing them with the household items they will need in their new role as wives. The impression one gets from the suggestions on how to do this would indicate that the women may want to take on a feminine role involving domestic duties, but their experiences in Russia will not have prepared them to shoulder this role technically, even if culturally they have been taught that it is their duty. So the Internet sites suggest ways the men can make this transition easier and stress that the men need to show their ladies *how* to operate the domestic appliances they will be expected to use. The stove apparently does not cause a new Russian bride too many problems, and the dishwasher and garbage disposal can be learned with a little patience, but laundry facilities are another thing entirely.[13] Considering the fact that in all my time in Russia I met only two families that had washing machines at home, that laundromats do not exist in any but the most urbane environments, and that nearly everyone washes clothes by hand in the bathtub, this should not be such a surprise. But to judge by the way the subject is broached on the Internet, it seems that most men are a little taken aback by their wife's lack of familiarity with washer-dryer technology.

Hand in hand with teaching the woman how to use the household appliances, and thereby turning over the domestic responsibilities to her, the men are also warned that they may suddenly feel as if they no longer have control over many of the practical things in their home. For example, they may discover they no longer know exactly where to find things anymore. "You may find your lady will rearrange your entire home. You may find towels located with the trash bags and furniture polish, your pantry filled with food and laundry detergent, fingernail polish and a variety of other non logical items."[14] This is chalked up to cultural differences between Russia and America, and the fact that American homes have more specially designed closet space, which Russians are not used to. It is presented as one of those quirky little habits the men should tolerate and try to find endearing, but, at another level, this advice really addresses the adjustment process the men go through.

The woman's English skills, or lack thereof, can also cause the couple problems in the early days of their relationship. Although these couples have been able to convince the U.S. embassy that they have fallen in love and communicated through their letters and the obligatory visit to Russia, it appears from the advice sites that most of them experience problems with language when the women first arrive. The sites suggest being patient with the woman and giving her six to eight months to learn English. During this time problems with communication need to be dealt with by the man, and tips on how to do this abound. Above all, the sites suggest enrolling the woman for English lessons if the man can afford it. And if private lessons are too expensive, the men are advised to ascertain what sort of community education classes exist for immigrants in their area. While the women may be able to read and write English, pronunciation and understanding can be difficult, especially since even though American English is gaining ground in Russia, many Russians have learned British English in the schools, particularly the older women.[15] One of the women I spoke with, who is very active in Internet bulletin boards for Russian brides in America, concurred that language problems are one of the biggest stumbling blocks for many women. "They are so brave," she said of the women who move to America without really speaking the language. "But they probably don't realize what sort of problems they are going to have." This is especially true of the women who find their way to the Russian language-based Internet bulletin boards in search of help dealing with abusive husbands. "The women are advised to call the police if there is some violence at home. If there is abuse, then try to get to a shelter," she explained to me. "But how can they call 911 if they can't speak English? How can they explain why they are calling?" She said that she would recommend that women make an effort to learn English well before moving to America. But not everyone does.

For those who don't, paying for English lessons is obviously thought to be worth the money. And, as one site claims, "It's much easier to teach English to a Russian lady, than to teach an American woman how to be a good wife."[16] I'm not sure if that quote is meant to imply more about Russian women's perceived language skills or American women's willingness to be "good" wives. Or perhaps the quote speaks most loudly about some men's expectations of what a good wife is—one who cannot speak back.

Many sites suggest that technology can be used to help the women learn English while at home. They predict that the new wives will enjoy watching daytime TV, especially talk shows, because that is one way they can keep up with fashion (or alleviate boredom, though that is not mentioned). The women may also find a bit of home in American talk shows. One of the most popular TV shows in Russia is *Ia Sama,* a talk show that discusses everyday problems with featured guests and usually ends up centering on male-female.[17] Watching the American counterpart to *Ia Sama* on TV could be a way of dealing with homesickness. However, at first it can be difficult for the women to understand what is being said on the TV, which is not surprising considering the colloquial dialect of the average *Ricki Lake* guest. To deal with this problem, the men are encouraged to figure out how to activate the closed captioning feature on their TV so the women can read and hear the English at the same time, and to rent DVD movies with English subtitles.

Language problems can also complicate the process of introducing the woman to her husband's family. Meeting one's future in-laws can be a stressful event, anyway, but for a person who does not speak the language, it can be even more difficult—especially if the in-laws are slightly skeptical about the way the couple met, as some people may be toward mail-order brides. One site suggests that the men should, "try to keep the introductions light in conversation. Let your Russian girl move at her own pace. After a bit of time she will probably loosen up and initiate conversations of some sort even if it is asking everyone if they would like something to drink."[18] This site also suggests diffusing at least the language difficulties by bringing along a photo album of the woman's life in Russia, which offers good topics for conversation since pictures from home are something the woman can talk knowledgeably about, and photo albums are a traditional way of breaking the ice with new people in Russia. It was a photo album, for example, that Natasha showed me the first time I visited her, the day we ate the chicken soup.

Having left her family and friends back home, the sites warn, a Russian bride may feel homesick. Dismal stories abound from men whose brides spent the first two weeks crying every day. So the men are encouraged to find ways to make the distance to Russia seem smaller and communication with her family easier. One suggestion is to stock up on pre-paid calling cards to make the long-distance conversations home affordable. Another option is for the men to purchase a computer for the woman's family in Russia and set it up for them in advance of her move to America. This way the woman can communicate with her family frequently by e-mail or chat without running up expensive telephone bills. Likewise, if the computer is set up before the woman leaves, she can use it to communicate with the man while they are waiting for her visa to be processed, which will also give her and her family time to get accustomed to the technology. In addition, the men are told to "Russify" their computers before the women arrive; that is, they should install Cyrillic fonts before their brides arrive "home" so they can use the computer immediately without problems. A couple of the women I met were in touch with their families this way. Computer-based communication is obviously becoming a more viable option than it was in the late 1990s, but it still needs to be made flexible. One woman I met, for example, achieved this by bringing along her Cyrillic keyboard so that she would be able to touch type in Russian.

And, of course, the sites also give suggestions for what to do if the woman has children, as many of them do. The men are encouraged to think about everything from making sure there are places for the children to sleep when they arrive (one can imagine the signal that not having a bed for the child would give) to having some games or toys for them to play with, and checking with the local schools to find out ahead of time what documents children will need in order to register for classes.[19] The men are also told to look for local programs designed to integrate new immigrant children into the community. Surprisingly, the topic of children is usually only summarily dealt with on the Internet sites, but from the interviews I did, it seems that the presence of a child and how well that child is integrated into the new culture can make a significant difference in how successful the marriage will be. The child's age and gender and whether the man has children of his own are important factors that influence the integration process for both the woman and her child, but they are seldom discussed in detail.

Like the women, children can find the new language that they are suddenly forced to use for school and friendships very difficult to learn. However, when I spoke with an ESL (English as a Second Language) teacher about the problems Russian children have adapting to their new homes, she said that the children of mixed American-Russian marriages have some advantages compared to children from other immigrant families because there is an American parent in the household. Apart from there being a natural source of homework assistance, this probably means that English is spoken daily in the home, and the child is exposed to English outside his or her classes. But perhaps more importantly, the child has a parent in the home who is familiar with the American education system. This parent can advocate for the child in the school system, ensuring that the child gets the help he or she needs, and can speak with teachers to introduce specific issues and smooth over conflicts. The American parent's familiarity with the system also helps in other ways. One couple I spoke with, whose child was a junior in high school, said that back home children decide about going to college during their senior year of high school. But in America, if a child plans to attend college, there are exams, preparatory classes, and even preliminary interviews that need to be taken and initiated during that child's junior year. Had it not been for the American father's understanding of the system, the family would not have known about these differences and their child would have missed out on many of the first steps toward a college education.

When it comes to learning English, how old the child is when he or she moves to America makes a difference, though, surprisingly, the ESL teacher said that it was not necessarily better for a child to start learning English at a very young age. She said that the ideal for an immigrant child is to maintain proficiency in his or her native language while also picking up English, thus becoming bilingual instead of replacing the first language with a second. An older child who is already literate in his or her mother tongue will have a better chance of maintaining that proficiency. Even though younger children can often pick up the American accent very quickly and give the appearance of being fluent much sooner than older children, there is a risk that since these younger children have not first become literate in their native language, they end up never being fully proficient in it. This makes a strong case for providing private instruction in the native language to children, even if that is what they speak with their mother. And, most importantly, children need to be able to feel comfortable, accepted, and relaxed in their new environment so they can dare to make the mistakes that learning a new language entails. Helping them to make new friends, through school, sports, after-school activities, church groups, or other youth organizations is particularly important.

In the end, though, the children tend to adjust to the new culture and the language quite quickly, and many of the problems that can occur during the adjustment period seem to be of the same sort that stepparents and stepchildren have in most new relationships, when the child suddenly has to compete with the new husband for the mother's attention. The one exception to that generalization is that expectations of what the child should do around the house are apparently very different between Russian and American cultures. Many of the men who have brought over wives with children are surprised by how little the children are expected to contribute to household chores. While the man may have been impressed with his Russian lady's ability to spoil him by taking care of the laundry, cooking, and cleaning, the spoiled children are not as entertaining. This tends to be chalked up to the *babushka* phenomenon in Russia, where there is often a grandmother who does the majority of the household work and the child is not expected to help out, as well as the fact that most Russian families have only one child. This situation is discussed on the advice sites for men as something to be aware of and guarded against. And while I am not sure how much more spoiled Russian children are than American children, it is true that the *babushka* phenomenon is prevalent in Russia. Especially after the shift to a market economy, child care has become relatively more expensive and privatized daycare facilities are unaffordable for many families, so many Russian women are even more dependent on their mother's help than before.[20] This lack of a *babushka* impacts the household in America, and also the women, emotionally. Not having their mother around when they moved to America can come as a big shock, and many of the women claim that it is their mothers they miss most.

When I was reading through the discussion groups and advice columns for the new Russian–American couples, I was struck by the way Russian brides were sometimes talked about as if they were helpless objects to be taken care of by the men, like children or pets, rather than tough and capable adults and equal partners in a relationship. One site's discussion of using Internet technology to communicate with the woman's family back home once she was in America gave the impression that the women were almost as vulnerable as teenagers on a foreign exchange program or young children sent away to boarding school: "Yes, she'll still need to make a lot of phone calls home the first few weeks but a scheduled instant messenger chat session everyday to her family will be a great help in reducing the frequency and need for expensive calls home and ease her homesickness."[21] On the other hand, homesickness probably is a problem for most of the women. Several women I spoke to brought it up without prompting. And one couple, aware that the woman was going to feel homesick and isolated during the long days in a suburban home while her husband was at work and her son at school, even went through the cost and hassle of importing her cat so she would have some company, as well as tracking down distributors of ethnic foods and beverages. So while the tone in the websites' messages is a little patronizing, the sites do offer potentially useful guidance.

Likewise, the suggestions for how to help the new wives figure out household appliances can be interpreted as either incredibly condescending or as practical, necessary tips for adapting to a new culture. Or both. It's hard not to see this language, for example, as demeaning: "Unless you sit down and teach them how to use some of these items they will never know [how to do it]. All of the instructions are in English and not every modernized household appliance is affordable in Russia."[22] But its observation is probably true in many cases. The women, especially the ones with limited English skills, need someone to show them how the technologies work, and their husbands are probably the ones best suited to do this.

I came across this same patronizing yet informative tone in the way the sites suggest certain safety precautions that may be wise to take. These precautions seem like the kinds of things one would help a child with, not a grown woman: for example, collecting medical and emergency supplies in one place and going through the various containers of aspirin, antiseptics, bug sprays, and Band-Aids with the woman so that she knows where and what to get in the case of an emergency. Yet, for those women who are not overly familiar with written English, especially medical terms and American brand names of medicine, this surely is a good idea. The same site suggests writing a list of emergency telephone numbers to keep close to the phone, including the man's work number and contact details for his relatives. And even more fatherly, though probably also useful, is the suggestion to write a "help letter" explaining that the woman does not speak English and giving the husband's address and phone number. The site suggests that the woman and especially her children could carry the letter with them if they decided to venture out alone. And as disturbingly similar to a dog tag as such a letter is, and as clear a statement that "this woman [and child] belong to me" as it makes, the letter is a precaution that someone lost and not able to communicate in English would possibly need. It may just be that the patronizing tone of some of these suggestions stems from the fact that when the women move to the new country, they suddenly find themselves in a situation that demands they rely on their husbands for help with the small, everyday things they would otherwise have handled blithely on their own in Russia. Changing cultures puts people in situations they do not understand (I think back to my experiences with the outdated rubles), and moving into a country without being able to speak the language makes dealing with these differences even more difficult. In some ways the women are very lucky to have men who are willing to help them through the transition, because everything around them can seem very different. Yet here, again, there is a caveat to add. The women I spoke with in America seemed to have husbands, and in some cases extended American families, who were consciously and patiently helping them through the transition. But I am not sure this is always the case. Some women can find themselves in relationships with men who are neither willing nor capable to help them adjust, and these women can become very isolated.

The isolating effects of cultural differences are probably compounded by material aspects of American society. For example, the transportation infrastructure in America is very different from that of the former Soviet Union, where many people do not have cars and are perfectly capable of leading normal lives without them thanks to public transport. In most parts of the United States, however, a car is necessary, something a lot of women are not prepared for. Many of them cannot drive when they come to America, nor do they have access to a car if their husband takes it to work, and they find themselves stuck in the suburbs or a rural area without being able to get around on their own.[23] One woman I spoke with said that not being able to drive at first was hard, partly because she could not do things like pick up her son from school to allow him to participate in any after-school activities, partly because she really missed interacting with the crowds of people she was used to back home, and partly because she could not just drop in on her American neighbors unannounced like she had done back home. "In our culture you can come to your friend's house without calling, and just say 'hello, I have the chance to come and see you,' but it is not appropriate to do that here," she told me. It also took a while for her to get accustomed to the lack of sidewalks where she lived. "I can't walk places," she said when we spoke. "I can't see or meet the people . . . in Ukraine, it is easier to see the people on the streets, but here it is just all cars. I like to be in the crowds and see the people, but here, even in the smaller cities, all the people are in their cars."

Luckily, this woman's husband had paid for driving lessons before she left Ukraine, and then she took some private lessons once she was in the States. She even tried driving with her husband, though that was a disaster.

"It was the worst. I thought we could kill each other," she said good-naturedly, laughing. She then confided, "One woman I know said if you have not gotten divorced after this you will pass the test and your marriage will survive." It may say a lot for the future of her marriage that she was able to pass the driver's exam on her first attempt. At this point she can see crowds of people when she goes to the shopping mall.

How much the husband can help the woman in all situations, though, is a matter of debate. This becomes especially clear around the issue of clothing, one of the most complicated aspects of the women's assimilation into American culture. The men are warned that their new bride is going to dress differently from and be more sexy than the average American woman. And from the online testimonials about how wonderful Russian women are, this seems to be one of the things that attracts the men to them in the first place: the observation that most of the women they meet while traveling in Russia look like models. They are thin and made-up, they dress in short skirts, and they "take care of their appearance." As one site says, "The Russian woman likes to look pretty. She likes to dress well when she walks in the city street to her destination. She wears a dress and pumps, or a suit with a blouse and jewelry. She is concerned about her weight, her hair, how she presents herself. She thinks gym clothes are for the gym."[24] This insinuation that American women think gym clothes are fine outside the gym appeared on many different sites, some not even insinuating but stating straight out that Russian women are better than American women because they do not wear sweats and baseball caps everywhere they go. But this Russian way of dressing, which looks so good in Russia, appears out of place when the women are in America. The "tight-fitting" fashion in Russia suddenly looks like hooker clothes in America. Acceptable color combinations are different in Russia, and the made-up, "taken-care-of" look with heels and dresses comes across as inappropriate in American grocery stores and suburban homes. The websites warn that even if the man does not mind, his bride will eventually realize that she stands out in the crowd and will want to buy some American clothes.

Helping her do this can be a challenge for her new husband, and the men are advised to try to find another woman who can take their lady shopping. Yet having a man willing to help her adjust her tastes and styles so she blends into the new culture is a valuable thing. Several of the Russian brides I spoke with mentioned how grateful they were for their husband's help. At the same time, however, the Russian women I have met have all been incredibly self-reliant. It can't be easy for the man introducing a woman into American culture to find the right balance between providing the necessary help to get her adjusted without insulting her pride and overlooking the survival skills and unique personality traits the woman has. And for both the men and the women, there must be an underlying tension in determining how much the bride should adjust to American culture and styles and how much of her special Russianness she should keep. After all, the fact that she is Russian is what attracted the man to her in the first place. Adjusting those "wild color combinations that no American woman would try" has to be balanced against the probability that the woman has attracted her husband specifically because she is not an American woman.

This conflict of ideals does not seem to be problematized much by the advice sites, however. Instead, there is a pronounced attempt to get the Russian bride to become like an American woman, with tips on how to deal with her stubborn refusal to change her ways. "Your Russian lady [. . .] may resist some changes. It depends on the lady. Give her time and help her understand the American way. Do not force it on her but explain it to her and let her go at her own pace. Eventually she might change her ways but it's like anything else with a woman. It has to be something they want to do. Not something you are telling them to do. The more you can have your lady interact with other ladies the faster you will see her embrace the American way. You might say it's a woman thing."[25] What confounds me about this advice is that the men were looking for Russian brides specifically because they did not like the women they found in America, but that seems to have been forgotten somewhere around the airport customs and passport control.

To some extent, the women adapt to their new culture regardless of the man's influence. The way one woman experienced these changes is detailed by Elena Petrova, using her own insight into Russian culture and her own experiences of adapting to the West once she was married.[26] Writing about the efforts Russian women make to look beautiful, Petrova says that when she first moved to be with her husband she also looked like a fashion model. But after a while, she adapted to her surroundings and started wearing jeans and tee-shirts, just like the other women in her new home. And she stopped wearing as much make-up as she had. At that point, she stopped looking particularly Russian and started looking like the other women around her.[27] It has been argued that Russian women spend so much time on their appearance as a response to the enforced depravity and blandness they endured during the Soviet era,[28] though I am not sure I concur with that theory. It seems to me there is just a great deal of social pressure on women to try to look young and beautiful in Russia, and, ironically, somewhat less pressure in the United States, despite what is streaming out of Hollywood, on the TV, and in the beauty magazines. This Russian emphasis on youth and beauty can be seen, for example, in the fact that calling an older woman a "girl," *devushka,* is a compliment, while calling a woman a "woman," *zhenshchina,* is not considered polite.

I think this linguistic note is revealing. It is also probably one of the reasons most of the websites about mail-order brides use the somewhat antiquated term "ladies" when describing their product. "Women" would not really sit right with their Russian clients, but "girls" sounds a bit inappropriate for their English-speaking audience. "Ladies" is a compromise, and it has spawned the use of the otherwise antiquated "gentlemen" to refer to the men.[29] Yet, whether they are called women or girls, and whether or not they are wearing make-up like a Russian, the rhetoric still claims that Russian women are different from their Western counterparts, even if they end up looking very much like them after some time in the States. "The main difference is that they are much more patient and can tolerate things that Western women will never be able to bear. They are more considerate and dependable. They are partners, not competitors."[30] One can only assume that the men do not want to change this aspect of the women's Russianness.

Demeaning as some of the advice on these sites may sound, it is addressing issues of cultural difference and cultural shock that are very real for the men and for the women when they first arrive. One woman I spoke with said it took about a year before things really calmed down after her move and she and her husband stopped being continually surprised at what the other person did. "But," she said, "it still happens sometimes that we misunderstand each other and ask, 'why did you do that?' . . . like once a week. And you have to deal with that. I believe that in the good families, both partners try to understand each other."

This was also the case for Marina. And even though her husband was there for her, helping her figure things out and buying the bacon and bread she missed from the Russian import store, for some things she relied on other women in her circle of friends, and her mother-in-law was very helpful, especially for learning how to interact in American culture. In the beginning, Marina would be taken aback when people she did not know very well asked her questions that she thought were too personal. But Wendy told her that she was just going to have to get used to that. "People here are friendly," she said. "And that's just the way people are. They talk about everything." She also tried to help Marina with her English, an area in which advice can be frustrating to get from the man to whom one is trying desperately to communicate an intimate thought or feeling. "I've learned that Russian doesn't have any articles, which is why she doesn't say 'the' or 'a' sometimes," Wendy told me. "So I've had to try to teach her about articles, and some of the pronunciations. I tell her to hold her mouth a certain way and put her tongue in a certain shape, and then she can do it . . . When she asks for help, that is," Wendy said after a brief pause, giving the impression that help from a mother-in-law can be tedious at times. And like Anya's demand of Olga, Wendy has told Marina that when she and Robert have children she should speak to them in Russian, so the children can communicate with their maternal grandparents. In the meantime, Marina speaks Russian to the family dog, which is quickly becoming bilingual.

Like the other Russian women who have moved to America, Marina is gradually learning to live in America and still be herself. It has not always been easy, and it takes some time. This balancing act means thinking about how much to tap into local pockets of Russian immigrants. How does one strike a balance between buying Russian groceries and maneuvering in the large American supermarkets like one's American neighbors? When is one an American wife and when is one a Russian woman married to an American man? The Russian wives are both inside and outside the Russian immigrant communities in America, which is probably why some of the brides become active in the Internet-based chat rooms for Russian women that have sprung up through the already existing chat rooms for American men. Here they can communicate with other women who share their dual identity as a foreigner and a member of an American family. In any case, solutions to all these issues are determined on an individual basis. Just as the women I met in the former Soviet Union were each approaching their correspondences in their own unique ways, so too do the women negotiate their positionality as Russians in an American household differently.

"Marina had the most problems when she was trying to be an American woman," Wendy told me at the end of our interview. "But you know, my son liked her because she wasn't an American woman. She was old-fashioned. And she had said that in her bio; that she didn't want to be liberated, that she wanted to be spoiled with chocolates and flowers. That's what he liked about her." In the end Marina has decided to be what she is: a very Russian woman living in America. And this is something all the women I spoke with were doing: creating a hybrid identity that balanced their Russian background and their American foreground.

7

Anastasia and John: Making a Marriage Work

*T*he last couple I interviewed is an example of what the women I met in the former Soviet Union were dreaming of finding. John and Anastasia live in a split-level house from the seventies, on a quiet street in what was an outer-ring suburb but has now become part of the urban sprawl of a large American city. Their home is newly painted and well kept up, and the yard is large enough for Anastasia's nine-year-old son to have plenty of room to play. When I spoke with them, it struck me that the "dream" they were living was very simple: a normal daily life filled with the compromises and rewards that a marriage entails.

John had started looking for someone on the Internet nearly five years earlier. He had been recently divorced and was working in a male-dominated field. Because he was not running into women he wanted to date, he had started searching for them on the Web. He said that at first he was not interested in Russian women in particular; he was mostly just using the Internet to find dates near where he lived. But then he got in touch with a man from Texas who had found "love" in Russia. This guy had been to Russia, fallen for a woman, brought her over to the United States, married her, and then divorced. But obviously he had been positive enough about the whole experience to go back and get another Russian woman as well as write a book about it with hints and suggestions for other men.[1] The Texan had also set up a website and a chat room, which John started frequenting, and eventually the idea of a Russian bride began to appeal to him. The Internet's chat rooms and newsgroups are known as a

forum for sharing information based on personal experiences, on everything from cars to medical problems,[2] and many of the men looking for
Russian wives use them to get personal advice from others who have
already been through the process. This was the case for John, too. "It was
in the chat rooms where I really got interested in finding a Russian," he
told me. "I was sick and tired of the women I met locally. A lot of them had
issues. But Russian women are different. I don't know if it has something
to do with the fact that they are very European, but they think that the
family can be nice. And they are beautiful. A Russian woman takes care of
herself and her family."

Before long, John was in contact with a woman from Moscow, and
even though he had never been to Russia, he figured it was worth making
a trip to see whether she was the woman for him. So he booked a flight
and a place to stay, wrote down the name of his hotel on a piece of paper to
show the taxi driver at the airport, grabbed his passport, and went to
Russia. He was a little shocked at the gray, dirty, wet city that met him, and
it turned out that he felt no emotional connection to the woman he had
been writing to, but he spent his time going to museums, Red Square, the
Bolshoi Theatre, and St. Basil's Cathedral. The romance did not work out,
but he still felt his trip was worth his while. "Though the technology there
was like something straight out of a spy novel," he added when he told me
about it.

When John came back to the States he was not particularly driven to
find a Russian again, but he was still a member at some of the websites so
he wrote to a few more women. He decided that he was going to be
completely honest about himself in all his correspondence and really let
the women know who he was. Eventually he developed a relationship
with another woman and they decided to try living together. So he flew to
Russia to meet her, she applied for a K-1 visa (the fiancée visa), and within
six months she was in the States. John said her visit was a nightmare. She
stayed about ten days and did not communicate with him at all. "She must
have been terribly homesick," he said. "She was just silent and emotionally dead." So they called it off and she went back home. John decided
he would try to find an American woman instead, not using the Internet
this time.

After about a year, though, John was still alone and he thought he would give the Internet one last try. He found five women he deemed interesting, four Americans and one Russian, Anastasia. "Dreammates is the site I found her on," he said. "She came from a small town in Siberia, and I found her by accident. I was finished dating Russians . . ." Anastasia seemed mildly triumphant when John said this. She had, after all, succeeded in making him change his mind.

"What made you decide to write to Americans?" I asked her after John had told me how they first got in contact.

"I wanted to find someone," she answered honestly. "I went to an agency in my city. You can do this from home, but I don't trust these sites for my computer, so I went to a social club for women who want to find someone. I gave them my photos and profiles and then I just waited for answers."

"There are lots of men looking for women," John filled in for her. "And some of these agencies put together romance tours, but those are a meat market. You meet lots of women, but that wasn't what I was after." I thought back to Vera's plans and was secretly pleased to meet a man who felt the same way I did about the tours. I found out later there are even people in the industry who agree with John's evaluation of the romance tours and introduction parties. The owner of one agency that specializes in customized matches for American men and Russian brides claims the tours are too much like wholesale trafficking in women. They also tend to invite problems, since the men spend a lot of money on the trip and think they deserve to get what (whom) they paid for.[3] But this opinion is not shared by everyone. Satisfied customer testimonials available on the Web make it clear that that some of the men do not object to the fact that the romance tours are a meat market.[4]

"I didn't know about this," Anastasia said, referring to the romance tours. Coming from Siberia, she would have been too far away to be invited to an introductions party in Moscow or St. Petersburg, anyway. "I just paid them some money and this agency, they kind of vetted the answers I got. They helped me understand the men who were writing to me. Like, they would say, 'This is just a game for this man; this one is kind of old for me; this one is kind of strange . . . 'They were helping me to write the letters, too, to translate them so I could put in my real thoughts. They charged ten rubles every letter, which isn't very much, but when you come to the agency, you have to pay for answers and for letters back. And I was getting forty letters a day, so . . ." She let me do the math and then continued. "And mostly it was strange people. I thought if this is just for fun and I'm not finding anyone, I'm going to stop. I didn't like the men who were writing me. There was always something wrong with them. Or sometimes everything was wrong with them. But then I got John's letter."

"What made you answer it?" I asked, thinking about all the strange letters Tanya, Olga, and Valentina had gotten, too.

"He sounded like a normal man," Anastasia said simply, as if that were enough. "He wanted real things. He dreams about real things. He didn't ask about sex and the size of my clothes, so I decided to answer him."

"I think we were both really honest in our profiles, and to me that was important," John interjected. "What I had been finding on the Internet up until then hadn't been successful. I figured, if I'm going to find somebody then they have to like me for who I am. I told her that I would be really honest with her. And I wasn't just interested in her body. When I saw her on the Internet, the only thing I saw of her was the shot of her face. She was smiling, and I just liked her words about how she was looking for somebody."

"I said that I want a man who loved me and showed this to me, and I will give the man all of my love," Anastasia told me. So she decided he might be the one and wrote back to him with a simple letter describing herself, her town, her life, and her dreams.

Reflecting on the first letter, John said it was nice, but sparse. "She just told me a few things in the letter. She didn't give up a lot of information, didn't ask about a lot. I don't know if this was due to the translating, but it felt a little like pulling teeth."

"I gave him my telephone number," Anastasia said, as if that could compensate for her short letter. "And he called me back. It was real to me, this was his voice. For me it was not so easy to find somebody who was real. I was beginning to think it was just impossible." Anastasia paused and then added, "We were just lucky."

John had written to Anastasia in the beginning of October. She wrote back right away, and within a month they had bought tickets to St. Petersburg for a ten-day get-to-know-you holiday. And this time John hit it off spectacularly with the woman he had been writing to. John told me that even though they had only corresponded for about a month, "I decided in St. Petersburg that she was the one."

He told this to Anastasia while they were there. "But I had to think a little about it," Anastasia told me. "He went home, and I went home, and then . . . then I said, 'okay.' "

The first two Russian women John met had been divorced, but Anastasia was only separated from her first husband. They had been living apart for three years, but she had never gotten around to finalizing the divorce, so she had to get that done before they could apply for a fiancée visa. Luckily, it was just a matter of paperwork and took only about a month, and while she was doing that, John started looking into how to get her the visa. Everything was much more complicated this time around, partly because following September 11, 2001, all U.S. immigration procedures became much more stringent. But it was also more complicated because Anastasia had a child to bring with her, though this was part of what attracted John to her. He has two children from his first marriage and they are an important part of his life. He wanted to find a woman with children so that she would understand how important a child is to a parent and be okay with his devotion to his children.

To ensure that all went smoothly, John decided to use a lawyer this time. "In February I contacted a lawyer who specializes in k-1 visas for Russian women. He has a Russian secretary, an office in St. Petersburg and Moscow, and one in New York. I found him via the other gentlemen from chat rooms."

The lawyer helped them figure out what documents to collect and told them to put together the photographs of their time in St. Petersburg and to get an international passport for Anastasia. They also had to get English translations of all the official Russian documents, including Anastasia's divorce certificate, and documentation of John's financial security to prove that he could support Anastasia and her son for the foreseeable future. Once they submitted all these papers and the application form, there was nothing to do but wait. And wait. First the application and John's status had to be approved, and once that was done "they" (the USCIS, or the U.S. Citizenship and Immigration Services, as the INS is now called after it moved into the Department of Homeland Security) did a background check on Anastasia to make sure she was not a terrorist. Only then was the application packet sent by courier to Moscow.[5] Months went by and they were still waiting to hear something, so John took some of his vacation time and they met up in a third country, Spain.

"We met in Barcelona that summer," John said. "Partly it was because we wanted to see each other, and it also helped us get the photos we were going to have to show at the interview."

"It took a long time to do the documents, and we wanted to see each other," Anastasia agreed.

Even meeting in a third country was not without its complications; a Russian passport is not as easy to travel on as an American, and American passports carry their own liabilities. "We had to find countries that she could get into easily—Egypt, Turkey, Spain," said John. "And we chose Spain because I didn't want to get killed in Egypt, for example. So we met in Barcelona. I had given her a promise ring in St. Petersburg, and I gave her an engagement ring in Barcelona. And we went to the Olympic park, the boardwalk, we went to a bullfight—which wasn't very nice, that we won't do again . . ."

Finally, in the fall, Anastasia was called to an interview at the American embassy, nine months after they petitioned for the visa.

"The man doesn't have to be there," John told me, but he flew to Moscow anyway. "In fact they don't even let you in. There is one little door on the side of the embassy for people getting visas, where you enter into a whole room of people waiting for their turn, and that's all the farther you get. So Anastasia and her son went in. It was mostly women and children there." Russian children do not have their own passports; they travel on their mother's, and the United States issues a K-2 visa for them, which is a large sticker attached to the woman's passport.

John took a deep breath to start explaining to me about the interview procedure, but Anastasia interrupted him at this point and began telling me what happened. "I was lucky," she said. "The woman at the embassy was nice to me. She spoke Russian, and smiled, and she asked me about

John. She asked me: do I know that he has children, that he's divorced, do I like him? When she asked me what I planned to do in America, I said I wanted to stay home, because this is a trick they do. If I say I want to work, to have my own business, then they don't give the girl a visa. They can trip up the women with very simple questions and then they will say, 'I don't think that you are really in love with him,' and the girl won't get the visa."

John agreed. He said that was one of the reasons they hired the lawyer. He helped them with the paperwork, and then Anastasia also had a pre-interview at his Moscow office to practice answering the questions they were going to get. "I have heard horror stories," John said. "Women who have sold all of their stuff, quit their job, and then the embassy says 'we don't believe you' and denies them a visa." For John and Anastasia it was worth the two thousand dollars. "He [the lawyer] has a woman in Moscow who did a rehearsal interview with Anastasia. And he knows the people at the embassy, eats lunch with them . . ." John let the sentence hang but Anastasia's experience spoke for him. She got her visa.

When John mentioned that the lawyer's fee was two thousand dollars, I was a little taken aback. But actually, estimates of how much it can cost to find, import, and marry a Russian wife range from three and a half thousand dollars or up, sometimes costing as much as twenty thousand dollars.[6] The initial costs of buying women's addresses may not be so high—they sell for as little as five or ten dollars apiece—but that is only the first step. Then come the costs of presents, flowers, telephone calls, postage for certified mail services, translating services, possibly a computer and Internet connection for the woman in Russia, the airfare for the trip over to meet her, plus the costs of visa fees and staying in Russia for the man, and the expensive application fees, official medical exams, trips to the capital for embassy interviews for the woman, her travel to the States, and so on. Once all those are added up, the Russian bride can become pretty expensive. And if the man decides to go on one of the romance tours or strikes out with the first couple of women, the process gets more and more costly. So after a man has spent all that money on a fiancée, not to mention all that time and emotional energy, the last thing he wants is for her visa to be denied. At that point, two thousand dollars really is not much compared to everything else he has invested.

Before we left the topic of their visa application, Anastasia came back momentarily to the questions she had gotten during her interview at the embassy, and the fact that she had been coached to answer meekly that she was not planning to work, just to be a housewife. She felt really insulted by this. "If there is a man and he wants to bring me in his life, that's okay, but the embassy doesn't want me in society," she said a little bitterly. "Maybe they are trying to prevent the gold diggers. And I think there are some, a low percentage of women, who come over to America and who are not very happy when they are here. These are the gold diggers. They will just sell themselves for money. I didn't do this because I knew that America was not a paradise. I just wanted to be far away from my old life and start over. And if John would be Swedish, or French, it wouldn't have mattered. Or if I would bring him to Russia, that would be okay, too. For me it wasn't the purpose of our relationship to leave Russia. In fact, I still have my apartment in Russia. For me it was to have John in my life."

"I think that is what makes our marriage successful," John agreed with Anastasia. "That there weren't false pretenses."

"But some women do this," continued Anastasia. "I had some friends in Russia who went to America and then came back. One woman, she went to be with a man and then returned to Russia. 'He doesn't have enough money,' she told me, and so she just left him. 'I will find somebody with money,' she said. And another girl I knew, her American marriage didn't work because they wanted different things, and they were both disappointed. But I know maybe four girls who left and are happy, two in the US, and two in Europe. They write letters back home and say that they are still together and they are happy. And one woman I know, she has spent one year in America already and they have some problems because of the language, but she says to me, 'I will stay with him here. You even have problems with your native guys in Russia, so it is like any relationship.' "

John listened respectfully to what Anastasia said and then returned to the story of their embassy experience. "I'd bought tickets home for us to leave two days after her interview," he said. "I just made the assumption that everything would be okay. But even if you get your visa, because of security you now have to have a DHL envelope, and they will mail the visa to you when they feel like it." So John, Anastasia, and her son spent the two days waiting in their Moscow hotel room for the DHL envelope that didn't come, and didn't come . . . With their departure time getting closer, they finally rang DHL and tracked down the envelope to one of the delivery service's offices on the edge of town. "We traveled across Moscow and had to walk about two hours to get to where it was," he said, "but we got the visa." And that evening all three of them traveled to the United States.

"Once you are in the States you have to get married," John continued. "So in January we were married in Las Vegas, and in February we applied for Anastasia's green card. They received the application in March, sent us a notice that within one hundred and twenty to one hundred and eighty days it would be processed, and now we've been contacted from the office in Nebraska, where they do the processing, that we've got an interview in April." I started counting the months in my head and worked out that it would have been over a year and two months since they applied for the green card before Anastasia was interviewed. And her fiancée visa expired after ninety days. So for most of that time Anastasia would have been living in America without a residency permit.

"My visa is expired, the driver's license . . ." she said, as if picking up on my thoughts, and John tried to explain.

"Her visa expired, and after 9/11 our state decided to make all official documents contingent on the visa, not knowing the problems that causes because the green card procedure is so lengthy." So when Anastasia's visa expired, her driver's license also became invalid. "Document-wise, yes she is illegal," John continued. "But we have all her papers, and a copy of the certificates she actually has, and the notice that they have received her green card application . . . It is only because the green card application is taking so much longer than it should."

"Can you work legally?" I asked Anastasia. I knew she was employed because we had arranged our interview around her work schedule.

"When we first came I asked for a work permit in New York, and they gave me a white card with an alien number on it. That will expire in May. I had to fill out a form and I got a social security number for work purposes, only." With her work permit Anastasia had found a day job at a bank and an evening job teaching aerobics, but she was still waiting for the green card. They started to tell me what they knew about their upcoming green card interview, and it sounded rather like a more detailed version of the fiancée visa application. They would have to go to the USCIS office in the state capital and be interviewed face to face. At that time they would have to show proof of co-residency; both of their names on bills, mutual credit cards, and so forth. And once granted the green card, they would have to go through a series of similar interviews for another couple of years. Only then, providing everything happens on schedule and after Anastasia has been in the country for several years, can she get a permanent green card.

Speaking with Anastasia and John, I could tell that both of them were intent on building a long-term relationship, not just procuring a green card and permanent residency. But even for those women who are only interested in a green card, several years is a long time, a lot of days to get through, mornings and evenings living with another person just to secure a permanent residency permit, especially since the application process is known for its delays. I shifted the conversation over to how John and Anastasia were communicating and making the adjustments to their life together.

"The biggest challenge is language," Anastasia said emphatically. "If you have this language it's no big deal. You can find a job, you can speak to your husband, read the newspaper, watch TV."

"If you can get past the language barrier you're about eighty percent of the way," John concurred.

"Do you speak Russian?" I asked John.

"I speak . . . ," John started to answer, and Anastasia interrupted him.

"No, he doesn't," she laughed.

"I know some words," John tried to make a comeback. "I can count, I know enough to be dangerous. I read a little Russian." But Anastasia just laughed. So I asked Anastasia how well she spoke English when she arrived.

"I spoke some English," she said, but in a way that gave the impression she had difficulties at first.

"She studied English at the university," John filled in for her. "And when we would speak on the phone before we met, she could understand what I said, but it was hard for her to answer. It was a lot of 'yes' and 'no.'"

"He was calling me twice a day," Anastasia interrupted. "I didn't speak a lot, but I could understand him. And he spoke slowly."

"He called you twice a day?" I asked incredulously, thinking I had misunderstood. But that was what she meant.

"He called me twice a day, every morning and every night."

"They were just short telephone calls, during the day," John added, but Anastasia would not let him belittle their importance.

"He was in my life every day," she said. "I knew that John would call me at eleven p.m., so if I was out in the evening I would have to drive very fast so I could answer the phone when he called."

"Now the truth comes out," John laughed at her. Then he tried to explain what he had done. "I went out and found a cheap phone card, something like three cents a minute to Russia, and I still ended up spending over three hundred dollars a month on phone calls. But I figured that if I had been dating a lady in the US, I would spend the same amount on dinners and movies . . . There were a few times she called me, and I loved that, but it was really expensive for her to call, so mostly I called her. Making a relationship like this work is a lot more difficult because of the distance. You have to overcome that." Obviously John's twice-a-day phone calls had been able to bridge the distance.

John and Anastasia could make themselves understood on the phone, but when she arrived in the States there was still much to be done with Anastasia's English. "I put her in English classes right away, and she did the whole thing in six months, and Alex did it in a year." John said, bringing the conversation back to language issues and Anastasia's son. "Alex could hardly speak English when he got here, and now he's losing his Russian," John said. "He can understand Russian, but when he speaks with his grandparents on the phone now sometimes he asks Anastasia, 'How do you say this in Russian?' He has soaked up American culture and language like a sponge. He just ate it up. He just accepted the fact that he didn't understand it, and it was no big deal. He's never gotten in any big fights . . . Well, he punched a girl once, more out of curiosity than anything else, just to see what would happen, but other than that I don't think he's had any problems. The teachers say he's very good in school." Anastasia agreed, proud of her son's accomplishment.

"How often do you call your family in Russia?" I asked her

"Initially I called them once a week, or twice a week, now maybe it's once a month . . . I didn't want to call when I first came here because I would cry when I talked to them. Now I like calling, I call during the day."

"Have you been back at all to visit them?" I asked, but Anastasia just sighed.

"She can't leave the country until she has a green card.[7] We were planning on going back this summer, but we don't know if she'll have the green card by then." John was obviously a little frustrated by the delay. "So instead we're trying to get her mother here this summer, but it is difficult to get a visa for her. That is one of the reasons why only Anastasia's mother is coming to visit. It will be easier to get a visa for her if her husband is still in Russia, because then the embassy will think that she'll return to Russia. It would be very difficult to get a visa for both of them to come."

"The American government treats Russia as if it is a third world country, like Africa," Anastasia said a bit bitterly. That was a complaint I had heard before, and to a large extent what she said was true. But for Russians, the comparison with Africa was particularly insulting, not least because during the Soviet period the USSR had been a geopolitical player in Africa, both giving aid to African countries and providing Soviet education for African students at Russian universities. To suddenly be treated as if Russia was comparable with Africa felt demeaning to Russians. To change the subject, I asked Anastasia what her parents thought when she told them she was moving to America.

"They said they wanted me to be happy because I had been preparing them for the move," Anastasia said. "And then, when I said, 'Guys, I am leaving in December,' I think they couldn't really realize it was true, up until the last day at the airport." But even though they were prepared, her departure was not without a few tears, and Anastasia's voice became slightly agitated when she spoke about the days just after her move. "The first time when we spoke on the phone, they were speaking about me in the past tense. 'Anastasia did this,' 'Anastasia said this,' and I said, 'Guys, don't speak about me in the past tense.' So now they don't do this."

Then Anastasia explained what else they have done to help with the adjustment. "We made them a video. And we made them a tape of us that we sent back to them, too. On the tape we sing songs, speak to them about our life, and they listen to the tape maybe every day. And now they say,

'Anastasia we just want you to be happy.' A couple of weeks ago, after watching the video, my father said, 'I haven't seen you this happy for ten years. You're quite different.' I smile more, I look happier."

I could tell that John was glad to hear this. "What did your family think?" I asked him.

"My brothers and sisters thought it was great. My parents were open-minded, they knew how sad I was and wanted me to be happy. My mother thought Anastasia looked a little gaunt when they first met her, but my parents love her. They think she's the next best thing to sliced bread. My mother's said she's never seen me this content. My parents are very Catholic and they want me to get my first marriage annulled. I don't have the motivation to do it right now, but they want me to. Maybe I will at some point . . ."

"What about the difference between being a Catholic and being Russian Orthodox? Is religion important?" I wondered, thinking about Olga's comments about religion and race.

"It concerned me," John said, and Anastasia answered at the same time that it was not a problem.

"No, as long as he's white, and he's Christian," she said. "I just believe that God is here but I don't have to prove this by going to church."

"I haven't been to church for a long time," John confessed. "I don't feel like getting out of bed on Sunday mornings. My faith is still important me . . . Actually, as long as she's open and doesn't degrade me, it hasn't been an issue."

"They pray before every meal," Anastasia said, referring to John's parents and pointing out something that most people do not usually do in Russia but which is common in much of America. "But it's not a problem. All the families [of John's siblings] are different. Some of them married Lutherans, they have me now, who is Orthodox. It's not a problem."

"What about culture shock when you first came over here?"

"I didn't have this culture shock that everyone talks about," Anastasia answered. "Maybe it's because our life is very similar in Russia." Then she proceeded to contradict herself and discussed the differences she had found. "Some things are I don't like here, some things I like more than in Russia. Like, life here is more comfortable, but you lack some fun stuff. You don't know how to celebrate holidays, for example."

"When they celebrate in Russia, they laugh, play games, drink," John explained. "They laugh a lot."

Anastasia agreed and pointed out another cultural difference. "Eating. It's the most fun thing for American people, food. In Russia we'll go to a restaurant and order a glass of wine and appetizer and listen to the music. Here they just eat. But life is more comfortable, more convenient in America."

"For example," said John, "in her old job it would take two days to pay the taxes, but here you just put your return in the mail, or pay over the Internet."

"But there is no personal contact," Anastasia countered. "My work in Russia relied on personal contact. I was a financial manager for a company, and teaching aerobics at night. But here I am a teller at a bank . . . It's frustrating to be only working as a teller and I know that the women I work with only have high school degrees."

John tried to explain her dilemma. "She has a BA in economics, but no one seems to respect her degree because it is from a Russian university. There are places in the States that will confirm what sort of equivalent degree it would be in the US, and we're looking into that. And we're in the process of trying to find out what schools would be good for her to get a master's in. We're looking at a master's in business. But now at least she's certified to teach aerobics. She just got her American certification for that."

Not getting professional acknowledgment for her degrees and work history from Russia was wearing on Anastasia. This is an experience common to many immigrants. When they move to the new country they often lose some of their professional and even social status and end up having to take jobs they would be overqualified for in their home countries.[8] But after John mentioned the aerobics, Anastasia's mood lightened a little. "You know, even so, if I could just bring my friends and family here I would be completely happy."

"Have you found friends here?" I asked.

"I think I have two friends from my fitness club. I hope that they're my friends, anyway." John reassured her they were.

"A lot of the women I spoke to in Russia seemed to be wary of American feminists," I said, thinking back to all the comments I had heard in Russia. "Have you found that American women are more likely to be feminists than Russian women, and that they're difficult to be around?"

Anastasia said no. "I think American women are more independent and respect themselves more. I haven't had any problems with them . . . But in Russia I never heard about American feminists."

"What about food?" I continued. "How was adjusting to American food?"

"It's the same food," Anastasia said, but John disagreed.

"Anastasia cooks differently," he said. "She opens the fridge and what's there she makes. Like, I've had parsley salad." Anastasia seemed surprised he thought this was weird. John quickly reassured her. "But it's good. I like her cooking. She cooks differently. Her method of cooking is a little different. It's healthy. Healthy is good . . . And she loves Chinese food."

"But I can't eat Mexican food. And there is more fresh food at home, in Russia. There I can buy milk only for two days and if I keep it any longer than that, it goes bad. This milk in America, you can keep it for months. At home we used to be able to keep yogurt for only one day. Here it keeps for a long time."

John sighed weakly as if a little exasperated. "It's the difference between sterilized and pasteurized milk. We've had this discussion before. Anastasia thinks some of the food is not healthy . . ." I could tell they had talked about this many times, probably in the dairy aisle of their local grocery store.

"What about housework?" I asked. I was wondering about Tanya's question and thinking that if the men whose letters I had read were using the phrase "care about the family" as a euphemism for doing the housework, their search for Russian women would be justified by cross-cultural research on housework and gender roles. Household labor is less equally divided in Russia than in the United States.[9] Having grown up in a culture that assumes housework is a woman's job, a Russian bride may be more willing to shoulder a larger share of the burden than her American counterpart. John had used that very phrase earlier in the interview and I wanted to know if he was thinking about the same thing. He hesitated briefly when I asked him about it.

"For the most part, it's true, Russian women do more than what the

American women do," John said, referring to the stereotypes. "But I know neat freaks in America who do more housework than Anastasia. I'd say that Russian women keep a better home. Not necessarily a cleaner home, but a better home. They're more concerned with the family. We had a big issue about this recently in our family. Anastasia feels that when someone in the family comes home you should greet them at the door. I hadn't thought of doing this, but it's nice. We do that now."

"And you have to see them off when they go," Anastasia interjected.

John agreed. "So it isn't necessarily a cleaner home, it's a better home. But the housework issue isn't huge. In fact, it's not really an issue. She could be messier and I wouldn't care. That's not why we're together."

Anastasia agreed with him and then John continued. "We have the same problems as any normal couple; we don't like each other's habits, that kind of thing," he said. "But you work on the normal problems. Once you get past the language barrier, you get used to the other person's habits. At the same time, if you're willing to go across national boundaries to find a partner, you're already aware that it's going to be different and you've thought about how you can adapt that into your life. It is difficult for the woman, and she has to adapt, but even her coming here involved changes for me, too. I had to go from being a single guy to being married and that was a problem."

Anastasia agreed with him. "At home the man has to take a very huge role to help. John supported me a lot. Even with little things it is important. Like watching TV in this language, you don't understand what they're saying and it drives you crazy. Sometimes I would just cry for no reason. But John, he helped me, he would speak with me, he would drive with me every place I needed to go, he would be here for me, he wasn't nervous, or angry, and he never got frustrated at my tears."

John added to what Anastasia was saying. "I did a lot of reading on the Internet and there the guys who had already brought wives over would talk about their problems. I went to Russian women's sites too, just to get more knowledge. And the main thing all these sites said was you have to be there for her. So if Alex got sick, I got off work, because it was easier for me than for her. And I don't leave her alone. There has to be a lot of emotional support . . . and someone who understands what to do, to explain some of the things that she didn't know how to do, things that to me are so simple and self-explanatory. And you just have to have patience and explain these to her. One of the biggest things, for example, was that she would call black people 'niggers.' It's normal in Russia, and it's not considered a derogatory name, but here it is, in America, and I had to explain to her that she couldn't call black people 'niggers.' And working at the bank she is exposed to black people and Asian people, and this means that she has had to adapt, not just to American culture, to other people's cultures, too."

At the same time that John was helping Anastasia adjust, though, he also appreciated the fact that she was different. They seemed to have found that balance between adapting to American customs and keeping the Russian aspects of her personality. "I like her accent," John said. "Her sense of humor is different, what she thinks is funny is different, how she sees things is refreshing. I try to keep an open mind to her thoughts and opinions. And sometimes I correct her, like I'll say to her, 'Okay, it may look this way but that isn't the way it really is.' But her values are different and her views are different. It has refreshed my life." John's words made it clear that he was glad to be with her. "I genuinely feel that she cares about me," he said.

"And he cares about me," Anastasia said warmly of John. "It could be great if he made more money, and I have to help with the household budget . . ." John laughed slightly.

"Yeah . . . And when she wants something done she wants it done yesterday, and we never have enough money." But they were laughing with each other and I could tell they were sharing a joke between them. There was love in his voice.

"Do you have any advice you would give other people trying to start a Russian-American relationship?" I asked them just before the end of our interview, and Anastasia jumped in with an answer right away.

"I would tell Russian women, 'Don't try to find a new place to live in, try to find a person. You'll hate this place if it is the wrong person.' When they write letters, and when they put their bodies on the Internet to sell themselves for money, it's the wrong idea. They should try to find a guy. They should try to imagine if it would be okay if he wanted to move to her place. Would she stay with him then? I think that if you don't want to have him in your home, or your city, you shouldn't start doing this. I think most of the girls who want an easier life, they get bad results."

"And the men have to be able to keep an open mind, too," John said, "because you can't expect Russian women to do what you can expect from a typical American woman. A lot of guys get upset about that. But Russian women are different. For example, Anastasia would wear very sexy clothing. She had a very sexy bathing suit, but over here the people at the pool make her put a towel over it. Her bathing suit covers all the places it's supposed to but still they make her wear a towel. So the guy has to be very accepting." John paused and then said lovingly, "I tell her sometimes that I had to go to the opposite side of the planet to find her."

"Yeah," Anastasia said, obviously glad he thought she was worth it. "And if John was a Russian man, I would love him, anyway. It's because of his personality. He's special."

With the comment about his personality, Anastasia underlined what she and John felt was making their American-Russian marriage work: they were approaching it the way a couple tries to make any relationship work—developing communication channels, accepting the other person's flaws, and making compromises in one's daily life. Arguably, they are recreating the power structures common in heterosexual marriages and these can be related to class, race, and ethnicity.[10] Doing so seemed to be a common goal for both of them, as it did for the other people I had met while doing this study. Of course, there are elements which are specific to the fact that theirs is a cross-cultural, American-Russian marriage, but in John's and Anastasia's case it seemed that their daily life was focused on producing and reproducing practices to develop a specific partnership between two people. That he is American and she is Russian is important, but perhaps not the deciding factor for success.

8

A Catalogue of Hope

*B*oth Olga and her mother had insisted that they needed to live in a city and would not accept a proposal from a man who lived in the provinces, an attitude which reflects a strong undercurrent in Russian society that looks down on rural life and considers it intolerable compared to life in modern, cosmopolitan cities. This desire to be in a city is an incarnation of the fact that people have been trying to escape Russian villages for years.

Close to the Finnish border, however, I met a man who gave the concept of escape an entirely different dimension. I had been invited to tag along with a friend on a drive out to a distant village in Karelia. He was working for an American timber company and had to meet some people to discuss a shipment; I was just glad for the chance to get out of town for a day and explore a different place. We left early and watched as the sun rose slowly, first making the snow appear lighter and lighter on the road, and then casting slashes of pink through the fir trees. As we drove out of the thick forest into the clearing of the village, around nine in the morning, the sun had finally climbed high enough to clear the tree tops and make everything glitter with the hoarfrost that had formed during the night.

I was dropped off in front of the village church while my friend left to talk business, and I slowly wandered down one of the side streets that was covered in a thick layer of ice and packed snow. Though I had seen a couple of three-story, concrete apartment buildings in the center of town, most of the houses were built of wood; two family homes with a small patch of garden around them and a wooden fence between the plot and the road were typical. We had driven through a dense pine forest to get there, but in the village most of the trees I saw were birches and poplars, all leafless and frosty against the cold blue sky. Pale pillars of smoke were lifting from each of the chimneys, rising straight up and dispersing in the still morning air above the different patterns of painted woodwork that decorated each of the houses, Slavic versions of the gingerbread that one finds on Victorian houses in the United States. Most of the houses had been painted in blue or green at one time, with the decorative woodwork in a darker shade or white, but they were all run down and in need of repair. I could see what looked like outhouses with fresh paths to them in the back yard of each house, and I suspected that the houses had only cold water on tap, if they had running water at all. But in the fresh white snow and soft pink morning sun they appeared warm and cozy. Even if everyone I had spoken to in town had condemned the villages as being backward, boring, and filled with aging alcoholics, on that morning, in that sunshine, the village I found myself in seemed to have materialized off the page of a fairy tale.

As I walked down the street I heard little except the crunching of snow under my boots. Hardly anyone else was out, only the occasional *babushka* bundled up against the cold, carrying an empty shopping bag. I thought I could feel their eyes checking me out under the knitted woolen scarves they had wrapped around their heads and tucked tightly into their buttoned coats, but each time I looked at them, they managed to look away before I could make eye contact. So I just kept strolling down the street, which appeared to end in forest about a half mile off in the distance.

I wandered past a few more houses, noticed that the crocheted curtains hanging across the bottom half of each of the windows were the same sort that I had seen an old woman selling in the market a few weeks ago, and then saw two older figures dressed in black and moving animatedly around something in the ditch a bit farther along—or as animatedly as people their age could move. When I approached and looked at them more closely I guessed that the youngest was at least seventy. The women were pointing at the ground, and I saw what they were discussing: a little black beetle that had somehow managed to make its way up through the ice and was crawling around distractedly on top of the crusty snow.

"It's a beetle, alive at this time of year," one of the women said to me.

"How very strange," I replied. As soon as they heard my accent, they stopped looking at the beetle and stared at me.

"You're not from here," one of them said, clearly indicating that I was stranger than the beetle. The whites of her eyes were slightly yellow, but her pupils were blue and they looked at me curiously. The other woman she had been talking to was also staring at me, and she picked up the sentence as soon as the first woman had paused. "Where are you from?" she asked.

"I'm American," I said. The part of the country I was in had been closed to foreigners until very recently, because of its military bases and its proximity to the border. When I had met people from there before, they had often said at this point in the introduction, "You're the first American I've ever met," and proceeded to try out a few words of English or ask me what I was doing in Russia. Not this time. Instead of commenting on my nationality or waiting for me to introduce myself, these two women started waving their arms in the air and yelling to an older man who had been poking at the ice a few yards away.

"Matti, Matti," they called to him. Matti was obviously slightly hard of hearing so they waited until he had come closer before yelling loudly at him, "*Eta devushka iz Ameriki!* This girl is from America!" He looked incredulously at me as the two women shouted the same thing to him one more time. As what they were saying registered, he dropped the stick, took off his fur hat and held it in his mittens over his heart. Then, slowly, he started to sing, "My Bonnie lies over the ocean, My Bonnie lies over the sea, My Bonnie lies over the ocean," he picked up speed as he reached to refrain, "O, bring back my Bonnie to me."

I smiled at him, slightly nervously, not quite knowing what to do with this greeting, when he started to speak in terribly faltering English.

"I am from America. My name is Matti."

"Hello," I said, deliberately speaking slowly in English. "It's nice to meet you."

"I am Minnesota living." He seemed to be searching for another word, and I was trying to fathom how a man in the middle of the Karelian forest could be telling me he was American. His pronunciation was very close to an American accent, but he seemed to have trouble putting words together into a sentence. I smiled encouragingly at him while he stumbled over what sounded like "I live Duluth."

"Come," the older woman, who turned out to be his wife, said in Russian. "Let's go inside. Matti, you can show her your photographs. *My chai pop'em,* We can drink some tea." She hustled us in through their gate and up the walkway. I took off my coat and shoes in the entryway of their house and followed them into a kitchen that smelled like fresh bread. The room was warm from the giant white stone and plaster woodstove that made up the far wall, a walled-in sort of fireplace about four feet tall. It had a couple of different iron doors: a compartment in which to burn the wood with a drawer under it to collect the ashes, and different ovens that would be hotter or cooler depending on their proximity to the wood-burning compartment. Except for the stone chimney that went up along the one wall and out through the roof, the stove stopped about three feet from the ceiling boards. I noticed this because as soon as we entered the kitchen, something moved on top of it.

"Who is here?" came a shaky female voice from a pile of blankets on the stove's upper ledge.

"It is an American," said Matti's wife while Matti disappeared into the other room to get his photographs.

"An American?" A gray head appeared out of the pile of blankets and pillows on top of the stove, and a pair of feet swung tentatively over the edge. The woman was wearing the loose-fitting brown knitted tights that the state-run department stores still stocked, cotton nightmares that bunched up at the ankles and whose crotch always wound up around my knees after a few short steps. But the stockings were warm and this woman was not walking much. The toes she had swung over the side of the stove were curled up with arthritis and they looked painful to step on.

"Lie back down," said Matti's wife. "You don't need to get up."

"I have to see the American," she said, and slid her way to the edge of the stove where a few wide steps led down to the floor. The bed on top of that stove must have been the warmest, coziest place in the whole village. I moved closer to the stove and offered the old lady my hand, helping her over to a chair at the table.

"You're American?" she asked me loudly.

"Yes," I said, equally loudly, and nodded my head.

"This is my mother, Anna," said Matti's wife while she stuck a heating element into the teakettle.

"Matti is American," the old lady told me.

I nodded my head, still not quite sure what was going on, and Matti came back into the kitchen. He sat down next to me, completely ignoring Anna.

"He. America," she said again, pointing at Matti. I smiled at her as if I understood and then watched as Matti put two photographs down on the table in front of me.

In halting English he explained what I was looking at. "This me. Duluth. Nickel bridge. Five cents to cross this bridge."

I looked at the photograph he was pointing to and saw a young boy, maybe eleven or twelve, standing in front of the lift bridge in Duluth. The cars in the picture could have been from sometime in the late 1920s or early 1930s. I had no way of knowing if the young face in the picture was the same as the old and wrinkled one next to me, but I supposed it could have been.

"I live Duluth," Matti managed to say again. Finding the English words he wanted to say eventually proved too difficult, and he shifted back to Russian. I leaned in close and heard him talk about how his parents had moved their family from Finland to Minnesota when he was six years old, and he had spent the rest of his childhood on the iron range, along with many other Finnish immigrants. Among other things from that time he remembered the opening of the new lift bridge in Duluth, and the five cents toll charged to cross it.

When Matti was sixteen, he and his older sister returned to Finland, to Karelia, to help build the "new society." Apparently there were a good number of emigrants who returned at that time, part of an exciting belief in the future of Finland and the socialist state they were going to create. But while Matti and his sister were in Karelia, the Finnish-Russian war broke out, and when it was over both of them were trapped on the "wrong" side of the new border. Matti's sister escaped overland, through Siberia, and then into Japan. From there she somehow made it back to America. Matti was sent to a prison camp in Siberia, stuck in the Soviet Union.

"They thought he was a spy," his wife said. "But he was not a spy. He was not a spy."

"I learned Russian then," Matti said.

"Yes, you learned Russian then," his wife echoed.

After several years, Matti was released and allowed to move back to Karelia. It was then that he met his wife, and he started to build a life with her in Russia. "I helped him learn Russian better," his wife told me, and Matti nodded. After World War II, though, Matti was sent back to a labor camp in Siberia, this time for allegedly speaking ill of the Soviet state. And again he was released and returned to the village and his wife.

"People were jealous of us," his wife said. "Matti never said those things."

"But since then we've lived in this village together. For a long time," he said, and looked at his wife.

"Yes. For a long time." She smiled at him and took his hand. "Matti turns eighty next week."

"*Da,*" he nodded at his wife. "Now I speak Russian," he said to me, and picked up the picture of himself in front of the bridge. "But I'm American." I looked at his eyes and saw they were wet from tears he was just able to hold back.

It is easy to forget that not so long ago Russia and the surrounding republics were the USSR, a country which denied its citizens freedom of movement between cities, much less the right to travel abroad. They were trapped in the Soviet Union, in a country they could not leave, in a system that required passports and permission slips even to travel to other regions. When leaving had been impossible, doing so was tempting. Now the women I met there are living in a mirror image of that restricted world. They are still deprived of the right to travel freely outside Russia, but today it is the restrictive immigration policies of the West that limit their movements. In such a system, one of the few legal migration options available is to move abroad as a wife,[1] and many are trying to take that chance. According to a study done in 1999, there were more than two hundred international matchmaking organizations working in the United States, connecting between four and six thousand couples each year.[2] The significance of this option for women who are otherwise denied visas should not be underestimated.

However, as Constable argues in her study of Chinese-American marriages, it is too simplistic to view international marriages only through the lens of migration or escape.[3] These relationships actually involve much more bidirectional travel by both the men and women than "migration" would imply. The experiences of the women I met support this argument. Vera, for example, had been back and forth between the United States and her home in the former Soviet Union. Valentina was planning a visit first before deciding to stay or not, just as Tanya had said she was doing. And for both Marina and Anastasia, their relationships had involved initial visits to the former Soviet Union by their fiancés. One of the other women I spoke with went back to the Ukraine with her child and her husband from time to time, and visits from parents to the woman's new home in America were also on the agenda for a number of the couples. When discussing migration, the term "transnationalism" is currently being used to mean sustained, long-distance connections across geographical boarders, and it seems to be a highly applicable concept in the cases I have described.[4] Migration has been construed as a single move from one place to another, but transnationalism implies that people (and ideas and things) can move back and forth between locations.[5] The term also suggests that people can be active in more than one society at the same time. This is not really a new phenomenon, but the speed and ease with which people can communicate and travel over distance has increased in the last decades. By examining the established and continual exchanges between places that migrants come from and move to, one begins to see how people, money, and goods, but also ideas, values, and understandings, flow *between* communities, not just from the sending to the receiving community.[6] The Russian-American relationships I've seen are the basis of increased and sustained transnational exchange rather than unidirectional migration.

While researching this book, I came across something else that made me pause and think about these relationships and what lay behind them. A few websites not only offered to sell men the names and addresses of Russian women but also gave the men the chance to list themselves in a paper catalogue that the companies published and distributed to women all over Russia. One of the companies even called its catalogue a "Western Men's Magazine" and for between 150 and 725 U.S. dollars (depending on the size of the ad and how long it would run) the men could get their picture and biographical details listed in the catalogue and distributed to thousands of "sincere, marriage-minded women from all over the world."[7]

This service first reminded me of Vera and her catalogue of men. She was probably right when she had asserted that the men were looking for a type of woman, not a specific lady, and that they would be happy to be listed in her catalogue. And the men who list themselves in the "Western Men's Magazine" proudly claim to get hundreds of letters from potential wife candidates. But what I suddenly started to wonder when I saw this catalogue was why the Russian men were not listed in similar catalogues. And why American women were not looking for mail-order husbands. Why were these groups not trying to meet over the Net?

One explanation could be that Russian men are just as horrible as the Russian women imply. If that is the case, then I guess it would not be surprising that there is little demand for them on the international market. Who would spend thousands of dollars to import an unemployed, wife-beating alcoholic? But just as my own experiences in America suggest that not all American women are as horrible as the men's letters claim, I can only assume the same is true of Russian men. The Russian women may actually have other reasons for making the slurs against their fellow countrymen that they do. Research on mail-order brides from the Philippines and Mexico has shown that the prospective wives from these countries are just as likely to state that local men are unacceptable and that they are, therefore, forced to find suitable husbands abroad.[8] There are different possible explanations for why the Russian women might be doing this; perhaps they are actually criticizing their home country and the social disarray in which they live by criticizing the local men,[9] using men as a scapegoat for more general frustrations. If the men are the "cause" of the difficulties the women have making a decent life for themselves and their children, then leaving the country "to find a better man" is a legitimate recourse, rather than a relinquishment of one's civil responsibility to stay and try to build a just and equitable society.[10]

Likewise, if the descriptions of American "feminazis" always wearing gym clothes and baseball caps is an accurate characterization of American women, then maybe there is a reason why American women are not sought after on the international marriage market. This is actually the discursive assumption that some of the official reports about the mail-order bride phenomenon are based on: that American women are not desirable internationally, and that American men are.[11] But even if this were, implausibly, true, there would still be no reason why American women would not be seeking a spouse rather than being sought (especially if they are as feminist as the men claim and thus accustomed to being the active subject rather than the passive, purchased object). If the women in America have the option to be the ones out there surfing the world for potential spouses, then there must be other reasons the international matchmaking patterns are the way they are. Because if not all American women are bad wife material, and not all Russian men are incompetent husbands, the question still remains: why are there so many Russian mail-order brides on the Internet and not nearly as many Russian mail-order husbands?

I think the answer lies partly in the rabid debate about what the mail-order bride industry actually is.[12] Some people assert that it is a legitimate matchmaking business, made up of consenting adults who know what they are doing and decide to participate of their own free will. The opposite view asserts that the industry is a cover for trafficking poor women from underdeveloped countries into lives of servitude in the West. As I read papers that supported these contradicting views, I began to wonder if maybe both were actually true. There is nothing which indicates they are mutually exclusive explanations, and I think it is quite possible that the industry is made up of consenting adults who know what they are doing at the same time as the international framework of inequitably distributed wealth and migration regulations are influencing the options available to these "consenting" adults.

The men and women who are finding each other through these sites are more than just "men" and "women." People are much more than gendered beings; they are also constituted by structures of class, race, ethnicity, and nationality, aspects of their identity which also influence who they are and what they do. Academic theories about gender have shown how people enact being a man or a woman, rather than assuming that the individual's biological sex is the determining factor in their gendered behavior.[13] I am not sure the Russian women and the American men importing them would agree with this way of conceptualizing gender, but the recurring theme that American women have been "spoiled" by feminism would seem to suggest that the men, anyway, can see that the gender role a woman assumes is at least partially influenced by the culture in which she lives. The Russian women who are desirable are enacting the kind of femininity some American men want, just as their American counterparts are enacting a kind of (un)femininity that the men do not want.

Those men, too, are enacting a masculinity which acts as a counterimage to the extreme femininity of the Russian women. Their dominant position in the gender hierarchy is a necessary component for the women to be able to assume a submissive (or docile, or noncompetitive, or traditional, or whatever one wants to call it) femininity. But the interesting aspect of this analysis is that both partners are creating their gendered identities. It is not something they are born into but roles they assume and enact in their letters, their telephone conversations, and eventually in their everyday relationships with each other.

Thinking about gender this way, as enacted in practice and defined in relation to the practices of those one interacts with, rather than existing in isolation and stemming from a biological sex, can help explain why mail-order spouses from abroad are nearly always women, and nearly always from developing countries, while the importing spouse is usually a man, and usually in an already developed country. I use these broader terms because the international economy of desire is not limited to American men and Russian women. The women I met had received letters from around the world, and mail-order brides come from many different countries. Neither is the movement limited to the traditionally assumed East to West pattern; the same thing can be seen with Taiwanese men who are bringing in mail-order brides from some of the poorer countries in Southeast Asia,[14] and with Korean, Filipino, or Chinese wives who are brought

into rural Japan.[15] The important point is that the existing gender hierarchy between men and women overlaps well with the hierarchy between
developed and developing economies. The hierarchy American men and
Russian women are creating through their daily practice of a dominant
male (or leading man, or head of the household, or decision maker, or
breadwinner) and the submissive woman fits well with the developed/
developing concept that pervades the international political and economic
discourse. The female in need of steering and direction is well aligned with
the developing-country role, transitional economy, and social instability
that Russians are currently expected to enact on the international scene.
And the dominant male also fits the image of the developed, industrialized
country which can share its wealth with other nations, as long as they
agree to adopt its ideas of democracy, capitalism, civil society, family life,
gender roles, and so forth. In practice, the partner from the developed
country in these relationships is in a more mobile and flexible position,
with English, dollars, and a passport that allows more unrestricted travel,
while the partner from the former Soviet Union is often dependent on the
other for visa support and possibly travel expenses.[16] At some level, the
power structures in the relationship are constructed by the bureaucratic
and regulatory hierarchy of international travel, economics, and, on a
larger scale, politics.[17] It is possible that it is less appealing for American
women and Russian men to place themselves within their prescribed
position in this hierarchy. The "dominant" Russian male may be less
inclined to assume the lower rung on the developed nation's ladder in an
international relationship, and vice versa for the American woman. Of
course, this explanation does not take into consideration issues of class and
race,[18] which also play a part in the building of relationships. These, too,
should be considered. As all these factors intersect in the relationships I
have detailed, it becomes apparent that the mail-order bride phenomenon
is about much more than men and women finding partners.

Neither gender roles nor national characteristics are written in stone.
That is the point of the theories about doing gender: because it is done in
practice, that practice can change. And there are certainly many Russian
women who are not submissive, a fact that has been observed by academics
and nonacademics alike,[19] contrary to the matchmaking websites' rheto-

ric. A country's place in the international order can also change, as Anastasia's complaint about the United States treating Russians as if they come from third world countries clearly indicates. But the relationship between men in dominant, strong nations importing women from weaker states with poorer economies, and the power imbalances that these personal relationships seem to strive after in the name of "traditional," "family-centered," and "old fashioned" values is hard to miss. However, thinking of the relationships in this way again reinforces the concept of a binary relationship of power between men and women and between developing and first world economies, as Schaeffer-Grabiel points out.[20] This is problematic because binary categories tend to offer simplistic explanations and hide the complexity found in the details of practice and context, complexity which the interviews I have presented here begin to display.

However, and perhaps even more important to consider, despite the underlying political economy of desire, the search for "love" is still a motivating factor for the people I spoke with, and one which is easier to articulate in discussions about individual relationships. Viewing the mail-order bride phenomenon solely through the lens of migration, transnationalism, and geopolitics misses what is perhaps the strongest force behind these women's attempts to find a husband in the West, namely, that they are trying to find a *husband*. Russian women today face social, political, and religious pressures to be wives and mothers,[21] but they face these pressures in a framework of economic and social tumult that limits their options. Trying to balance these demands against the desire to take control of their lives is very difficult,[22] especially for women who have been married once, are a little older, and perhaps have a child from a previous relationship. For them, and even for younger women who see the limited opportunities available for them in the former Soviet Union, finding a husband in the West is one way to take control of their circumstances while still being a wife and mother. By becoming a mail-order bride, or working with an international matchmaking agency, they can actively try to determine their destinies under a cloak of femininity, and thereby avoid being labeled a feminist and not a woman.

When I look back on it now, I see that the short, twenty-word descriptions I had read on the Web should have cued me to the fact that even if the

"Russian brides" were being presented as objects, the women behind the presentations were active and driven individuals with agency. They also had room to negotiate decisions in the process of finding a husband, at least as long as they were still in their home country. In addition, as I listened to the women talk about what they did to be placed on the Internet, I realized that their construction as objects was not only effected by the designers of the websites and the professional photographers who instructed the women how to stand but also by the women themselves. The Internet has provided a forum in which the women can be positioned as something to be purchased, replaying the gender and economic structures that augment sexism and misogyny outside of the Net.[23] But like the reproduction of gender structures in other contexts, in cyberspace all actors are implicated in practice, the women included. They did not describe what they did in terms of objectification, but they consciously manipulated the image of themselves into something which would be attractive to the men they were trying to contact.

This tactic has its risks, as the stories in American media about trafficked girls and abused mail-order brides attest. But it is important to note that as long as the women are in their home country, they are not in danger. It is the act of moving abroad to be with a husband that highlights one of the most difficult issues facing mail-order brides. Paging through the catalogue at Vera's office or gossiping about letters with a friend at the kitchen table, the potential mail-order bride is safe and secure in her own environment, enjoying the fun of being sought after by men she finds interesting and exotic, something she may not have experienced in her daily life for a number of years. But once the woman "finds love" and moves abroad to be with her husband, she loses the existing social network she had in her home country. She can become isolated in her new community, especially if she does not speak the language very well or has fallen in love with a man who is socially incompetent himself, overly protective of his new wife, or unwilling to let her work outside the home.

As if that were not enough, in most countries the woman is also trapped in a framework of immigration laws that force her to remain married to the man for a period of time or risk being deported from the country. The legal and social standing that these women assume when they cross borders and become a foreigner in a different land is what places them in potential danger. This is why the work of the late senator Paul Wellstone and Senator Sam Brownback, who fought for the Victims of Trafficking and Violence Protection Act of 2000, is so important, as is the International Marriage Broker Regulation Act.[24] These laws allow abused women to apply for permanent resident status without their husband's permission, provide background checks on the suitors to the women, and limit the number of fiancée visas (or fiancé, but male foreign spouses are conspicuously absent from the discussion) a man can apply for. Steps are now being taken, thanks to the new laws. However, it is also possible that the most recent legislation will shift industry practices toward more romance tours rather than simply address selling. The new law requires a marriage broker (mail-order bride company) to provide each man's background checks to the woman he wants to write to and attain her signed consent that it is okay to give her address to the man. This is considerably slower and more labor-intensive than sending the man an e-mail list of the requested and paid-for addresses. It would appear as if some companies are finding ways around this, but the long-term effects on the industry are yet to be seen. The law is also being contested in court.

However, even with new American legislation, the practicalities of getting information about American men to the kitchen tables in the thousands and thousands of gray apartment buildings throughout the former Soviet Union is no small task. I think of the women I interviewed and their dreams of a future, of a husband and a family, that they so generously shared with me. Those dreams were so vivid and stem from such an earnest longing to assume the accepted role of a "real woman," as a wife and mother, that I cannot imagine they would heed such warnings. These women's longing for a stable husband with whom to build a family is very strong. It is at least as strong as the desire the men have to find the perfect wife, one who is loyal and family-oriented, submissive, thin and beautiful, and preferably young. I thought of Olga's comment, "Sometimes I think these men just want to buy our youth." I had to agree with her. On the other hand, the catalogue of men that Vera showed me exists because some of the women are just as willing to buy the men's desperation, and to take the risks attached to finding a husband, a home, and a family abroad.

For the women I met, the letters they had written had varied outcomes. Olga and her mother wrote back to the suitor in Miami, but he never replied. Maybe he had written to another woman at the same time and that woman's letter was more promising than Olga's. Olga was not particularly sad about it, though, because shortly after we met she started seeing a Russian man from the university. Despite what her mother may have thought, Olga decided to marry him and she is still living in Russia, still married, and raising a little boy. Her mother is also still there, helping Olga with those household tasks she can, just like many other *babushkas*. I don't know if Olga has kept her collection of letters in the shoebox, but I like to think that they are tucked away somewhere in her mother's apartment, like a little box of childhood costume jewelry that can be opened up and fingered through in solitary moments of nostalgia.

Vera ended up writing to another man from her catalogue and after a short correspondence she procured a business visa through her connections with the U.S. matchmaking agencies and traveled to the States to try living with him. But for some reason he did not meet her requirements, and she was soon back with her mother and son, running her matchmaking agency. She has not managed to attract any serious attention to her idea about hosting romance tours in the city—it really is too small and provincial to be worth the trip for many men, especially when they can go to cosmopolitan cultural centers like Moscow and St. Petersburg. So she is still helping the women there find romance one letter at a time, and occasionally one foreign businessman at a time. And she is still getting letters from suitors who reply to her photograph on the Internet.

I don't know what has happened to Valentina. I did a bit of amateur detective work on Sam, the man she had fallen in and out of love with. I decided to find out whether the address she gave me was a prison or a mental hospital. It wasn't. However, it turned out that Sam was at least a little disturbed. He was neither a schoolteacher nor a secret agent, and he was writing to lots of women at the same time, lying about his identity. The way Sam toyed with Valentina and developed personal relationships with many women at once is not unique to men corresponding with mail-order bride candidates. Examples of this type of behavior on the Internet have been detailed in many different contexts, including men who maintain multiple relationships with women from their own country and within their own socioeconomic group.[25] So Sam was in good company, though "good" may not be the appropriate word. The police in Sam's neighborhood knew what he was doing because in the last few years they had been forced to take care of several women whom Sam had invited to come and live with him. These women, from different countries around the world, had arrived at the airport expecting to find Sam waiting for them. They all claimed to be engaged to him and insisted that he had invited them to come live with him. But when they arrived at the airport, Sam was nowhere to be found. The women were instead taken care of by the authorities until they could arrange for a trip back home. Each time the police had confronted Sam about this, he denied that he even knew who the women were.

The police could not arrest Sam for writing to women over the Internet, but they asked me to warn Valentina, so I called her back and told her what he was doing. I haven't heard from her since, and the phone number I have no longer works. I assume, and hope, that she took the chance and went to meet Wayne. And more than that, I hope that she has found a partner who offers her understanding and companionship. I hope that she has found someone to share her interests and her life with.

Contrary to everyone's fears, things went really well for Tanya. She was not trafficked into prostitution; she managed to find a job as a waitress, and within a year she found an American husband. At this point she is living on the West Coast, raising her own family. Her American family, that is. Her oldest daughter is still in the former Soviet Union, being cared for by her grandmother. But Tanya sends back money regularly to them, and they are all better off now than they would have been if she had stayed and tried to support them with the jobs she would have gotten there. Her courage and gumption make me suspect she would have found a way to succeed wherever she was, but what she has done has also broadened the world and created opportunities for herself and the people around her.

Marina and Anastasia both found husbands and made it to America, and Anastasia's green card has finally come through. They have both found jobs, and in time, perhaps each woman will also find a way into her new community and be embraced by a circle of friends in her new life to help ease her longing for those she left behind.

Six different women, six different starting points, and six different outcomes. But if there is anything they have in common, it is that the letters they exchanged with men were only the first step in developing the relationships they were looking for. In some cases it was a necessary step, in others just a sidetrack that was entertaining or engrossing for a while but did not lead to anything more. However, in all the cases, letters were only the beginning, and there was more work to do when the women started to develop the relationships beyond correspondence. In many ways, the letters were just small bundles of hope. But even the dreams and hope those letters represented were valuable to the people receiving them, the six women detailed here, and the many thousands of others who are writing to potential husbands. As a woman said in one of the first letters I received:

> I loved my first husband very much, and he caused me to change myself. I tried somehow to make him stay, to hold on to him, but nothing helped, and he left me for another, younger woman. And I was left alone with my grief. I cried a lot and suffered deeply. But time went by and the pain lessened. And I now want to have a family again, and a husband. But it is not possible for me to meet men who could fall in love with me *and* my son, who would want to create a family, so I turned to a company which arranged such acquaintances. My friend has been corresponding with a man from Oregon for a long time and not long ago they got married. I have only received two letters so far, and correspondence from them has not developed. But I hope that there will be more letters. I hope that maybe the same thing will happen to me.

Notes

Introduction

1. The term "mail-order bride" is controversial, and I want to apologize if using it offends any of the informants I spoke with. I realize that the relationships I detail here involve much more than the simple selection from a commercial market that the term suggests. At the same time, "mail-order bride" is the widely used layman's term for women who enter into relationships through correspondence in this way. To make it clear to a wider audience what the topic of this study is and to avoid ponderous euphemisms, I have chosen to employ the term in this book. But I also problematize it. And, perhaps more importantly, the material I gathered problematizes the term, not least in suggesting that mail-order husbands would be an equally appropriate way of describing the phenomenon.

2. This is a legitimate rate of return for this type of qualitative study with a subject that could be deemed sensitive. See Constable 2003 for a sample with similar proportions, though on a much larger scale.

3. One can question how representative this study is of the larger populations, but as Vertovec notes when discussing transnationalism, "While actor-centred approaches carry the danger of overlooking larger structural conditions, they have the advantage of emphasizing motivations, meanings and the place of people as their own agents in processes of change" (2004: 10).

1. A Catalogue of Women

1. See, for example, http://www.womenrussia.com; http://www.forrussianwomen .com; http://www.special-lady.com; http://www.anastasiaweb.com; http://www .russianbrides.com; http://www.loveme.com; http://www.russian-brides-club .com.

2. For more information about trafficking, see the International Human Rights Law

Group (http://www.hrlawgroup.org) and the Coalition Against Trafficking in Women (http://www.catwinternational.org).

3. Hardey explains that "the computer has been used to match strangers to each other since the 1960s, when an attempt was made to match individuals by comparing data derived from questionnaires using an IBM 1404 computer in the USA. This was later marketed as 'scientific' matching, and the use of information technology has gained popularity ever since" (2004: 208).

4. See Hardey (2004: 209) for a detailed analysis of Internet dating sites and the role authenticity plays in the relationships developed on them. See also Turkle (1995) for an early study of online sociability and the thesis that this type of interaction is popular because the relationships developed in them can be quickly, easily, and painlessly dissolved without the participants losing face.

5. Hardey 2004: 210ff.

6. For a discussion of this, see Coupland (1996: 202), who asserts that "dating ads are indeed circulated through technologies that are well-adapted for economic market transactions but they do not appear to have duped users into wholly marketized formats for their interpersonal dealings. The data, and especially the audio-recorded self-promotional follow ups to written advertisements, show that advertisers who have initially subjected themselves to the formulaicity of the written mode do also command resources to resist and undermine the process of commodification itself. Some facets of dating advertising, then, actually show people playing creatively with the structures of the media and reconstituting themselves as 'human,' de-commodified beings. To this extent, commodification can sometimes be only a technical constraint on the communicative range of dating advertisements and a stimulus to self-expressive creativity, rather than a persistent threat to late-modern identities."

7. Scholes 1997:2. In addition, unlike the mail-order bride sites with page after page of available women, in Western personal ads, younger *men* are more likely to self-advertise in newspapers or on the Internet. Jagger 2005: 95f.

8. The agents charged between eight and twenty U.S. dollars, or about one month's salary.

9. The same has been shown to happen with information about other migration options, for example, on how to seek asylum in the West.

10. This is changing rapidly with the spread of Internet cafes, and more women are likely to have access to e-mail and Internet surfing today.

11. See Schaeffer-Grabiel 2005.

12. This assertion, of course, assumes a linear developmental model with modernization as the final goalpost, a model which can be and has been problematized in the academic development discourse.

2. Olga

1. See Young et al. 1981.
2. Pleck 2003: 5.
3. Sweetman 2003: 4.
4. Brook 2002: 47ff.; see also Reed 2004.
5. Grammatically, the man in this phrase is allowed to be an individual, pronounced to be a man rather than existing in relation to something else. The woman, however, is termed "wife," indicating that she only exists in relation to her husband and her new role in society as a married woman.
6. Pleck 2003: 11.
7. In 1963, 74 percent of all American households were married couples, but by 2003, forty years later, that number had shrunk to just over 51 percent. Francese 2004: 41.
8. See Sweetman 2003.
9. "The official propaganda of the Soviet Era taught that feminists were women who hated men and children and the family; feminists were unattractive and aggressive." Waters and Posadskaya 1995: 364.
10. Susanne La Font writes, "The Eastern stereotype of a Western feminist is a masculine, domineering woman who hates men. Although many women lead their lives in ways most Western feminists would label as liberated (e.g. obtaining high education, achieving economic independence, and valuing their careers), most post-communist women are reluctant to use the term" (2001: 215).
11. Kay 2000: 267.
12. Veselá 2003: 109.
13. Veselá brilliantly shows this happening through close comparative readings of successive versions of *Cement*. Her discursive analysis of the changing character-izations of the novel's female characters underlines how "with the death of the modernist movement and the institutionalization of Socialist Realism in the early 1930s, as Marxism itself became more rigid and programmatic, gender relations too reassumed their traditional, patriarchal forms. For women, this primarily meant restrictions of their sexual desire and a stronger emphasis on motherhood. While this tendency was present in Marxist thinking from the beginning, with Stalinism it gained dominance and remained more or less unchallenged until the fall of the Berlin Wall" (2003: 107).
14. Veselá 2003: 112.
15. La Font 2001: 205.
16. Geneva Foundation for Medical Education and Research website (http://www. gfmer.ch).
17. La Font 2001: 206.
18. As the Hungarian feminist Eniko Bollobas explains in La Font's article about

women in postcommunist states, "The various benefits women enjoyed in the communist societies, such as full employment, free health care, maternity leave, and cheap abortion, only sound appealing to foreign observers, to whom these words have different and much more positive meanings and who may not know the reality of the quality of such services offered. In Hungarian—as well as Czech, Slovak, Polish, and Russian—these words sound pitiful, cheap, poor and gloomy, because that is the reality they evoke." La Font 2001: 205.

19. La Font relays the following incident, which has become a bit of an urban legend in the field of post-Soviet gender studies: "Croatian writer Slavenka Drakulic, speaking at the 1990 Socialist Scholars' Conference in New York, shocked her audience by holding up a tampon in one hand and a sanitary pad in the other. She asserted that the unavailability of these products in Bulgaria (where she had recently visited) was evidence of the communist system's lack of commitment to the emancipation of women" (2001: 206ff).

20. Valentina Dobrokhotova, quoted in La Font 2001: 203.

21. See Clements et al. 2002.

22. "The return of women to the home is widely perceived as an ideal worth striving for, even if it is not always realizable." Waters and Posadskaya 1995: 355.

23. La Font 2001: 212ff.

24. Ibid.: 214.

25. Petrova 2005.

26. La Font 2001: 205.

27. Ibid.: 211.

28. Gemzöe 1995: 32; see also Azhgikhina 1995: 11.

29. Jürna 1995: 15.

30. Ekéus 1995: 19. See also Barbara Entwisle and Polina Kozyreva, "New Estimates of Induced Abortion in Russia," *Studies in Family Planning* 28(1):14–23; and "More Abortions than Births in Russia—Health Official," *MosNews*, 23 August 2005 (http://www.mosnews.com/news/2006/08/23/abortionproblems .shtml).

31. Azhgikhina 1995: 13.

32. Pilkington 1992: 209.

33. See Pilkington 1992; Gray 1989.

34. My thanks to Dr. Betina Bock von Wülfingen for this idea. For further discussion of these terms, see Bock von Wülfingen 2005.

35. Waters and Posadskaya note that after the dissolution of the USSR "feminism was able to drop the derogatory adjective *bourgeois* with which it had been coupled in the Soviet era, but for most people this was not enough to make it a more attractive ideology. It was associated in the public's mind with 'deviant' sexuality. Feminism was understood by Moscow professors as well as provincial newspapers to be a synonym for homosexuality, a subject that liberals as well as conservatives found deeply alien and disturbing" (1995: 360).

36. My thanks to one of the anonymous reviewers of this manuscript for this suggestion.

37. See Hesford 2005 for a discussion of the history of the term "feminism" in America and its association with lesbianism.

38. As, for example, heterosexuality studies do; see Ingraham 1999 and Pleck 2003.

39. Petrova 2005.

40. Ibid.

41. Luehrmann 2004.

42. Hirsh (2002: 36) refers to a 1935 article by Iarkho in the *Russian Journal of Anthropology* (A. I. Iarkho, 'O tom, kak ne sleduet zanimat'siia antropologiei,' *Antropologicheskii zhurnal*, no. 1 [1935]:146–50), which presents the idea of the Soviet socialist racial hybrid.

43. The racial and national background of an individual was a part of his or her official identity as a Soviet citizen, written on the passport and identity papers. Soviet resettlement policies under Stalin, for example, often uprooted and moved entire populations of ethnic minorities. There is debate about whether this was done within a rhetorical framework of race or nationalism, since the Soviet break with and opposition to German race-based theory would suggest that the Soviet policy was primarily concerned with addressing "nationalist" tendencies rather than racial groups, and nationality was viewed as a social-historical grouping like class, rather than racial-biological group (Hirsch 2002: 30). The Soviet ideology embraced the idea that the citizen was malleable and moldable, and that regardless of race or nationality the state was capable of social engineering (Weiner 2002: 52). But, whatever the theoretical foundation of the policies, they served to define and confirm differences between the ethnic populations of the Soviet in practice.

44. *Central Asian Review* (1963): 8.

45. Kotiranta 2000.

46. Moore's comparison of Russian and American cultural studies addresses this. She claims that "Russia shares with the United States a characteristic that is often presumed to be uniquely American, which is a population that is composed of a diverse plethora of races, ethnicities, religions, and cultural groupings. The proportion of peoples considered 'minorities' closely approaches that of those who identify themselves as ethnic Russians, in itself a classification that is an amalgamation of previously distinct ethnic groupings. The concept of multiculturalism as a means of constructing national identity, however, is still a fairly alien idea in Russia" (Moore 2003: 93). There has been some recent scholarship examining the similarities between Russian serfs and American slaves and detailing the historical connections between African American activists and the Soviet Union. See Peterson 2002 and Baldwin 2002.

47. Petrova 2005.

48. Ibid.

49. Sonja Luehrmann discusses race and how the women will be treated in their new country: "Women in Russia seem to offer all the traditional values men used to look to Asia for, but fit more neatly into the racial hierarchies of the US, and may be less readily recognized as 'mail-order brides' when appearing with their husbands in public" (2004: 863). See also Sun 1998: A01.

50. The usually cited example of this notes how Italians, Poles, and Jews were non-white immigrants to the United States at the turn of the last century but have become a part of the white category now. Schaeffer-Grabiel's (2004; 2005) work also presents the flexibility of racial categories, noting the appeal of pale-skinned Latin American brides who can be both a source of new genetic material and pass as white in the United States.

51. Jagger 2005: 95f.

52. Petrova 2005.

3. Vera

1. Petrova 2005.

2. This duality of material considerations along with the desire for companionship is not unique to Russian women searching for foreign husbands. In her study of mail-order brides in Japan, Kojima (2001) notes that Korean and Filipino mail-order brides have often chosen to come to Japan in order to escape the social stigma of being an older, single woman (at twenty-five years of age) and to send remittances back home.

3. The average life expectancy in 1999 for Russian men was 59.8 years and 72.2 for women, according to Goskomstat, quoted in Ashwin and Lytkina 2004: 204. In comparison, 2002 statistics from the Centers for Disease Control and Prevention place the life expectancy at birth for females in the United States at 79.9 years and 74.5 years for men (see http://www.cdc.gov).

4. Goskomstat, quoted in Ashwin and Lytkina 2004: 204.

5. Kuhn and Stillman 2004: 136.

6. La Font 2001: 211.

7. Francese 2004: 41.

8. Bailey 2000.

9. Ashwin and Lytkina 2004: 189, 205.

10. Cubbins and Vannoy 2004: 185, 195.

11. It would be interesting to compare this to the marriage contract in other countries. I have a feeling gender roles are very rigid within marriage in the United States, as well.

12. Cubbins and Vannoy 2004: 184.

13. Ibid.: 185.

14. Divorce in the Soviet Union has been legal and common since the 1960s. Ashwin and Lytkina posit that a Russian man's public standing is determined by his

position at work, and his standing in the family is dependent on his role as a breadwinner (2004: 193).

15. Ashwin and Lytkina 2004: 195.
16. Rotkirch 2000: 112.
17. Ashwin and Lytkina 2004: 195, 199.
18. Ashwin and Lytkina 2004.
19. Fleming 1994; Osborn 2004.
20. Wyatt 2002.
21. "Europe: Russian Tax Hike on Vodka," BBC World News, 10 February 2000.
22. Fodor 2002: 380.
23. Ibid.: 381.
24. Kuhn and Stillman 2004: 132.
25. "Chance for Love," www.chanceforlove.com, consulted 29 March 2005.
26. Petrova 2005.
27. Wyatt 2001.
28. Elena Petrova, who also runs her own matchmaking agency, suggests that be-tween 5 and 7 percent of Russian women looking for a husband are successful (Petrova 2005). The statistics available to the INS and congress also suggest that about 4 percent of the women trying to find a husband are successful (see Scholes 1999), but the information these statistics are based on is very difficult to col-lect accurately, partly because not all couples want to admit they met through Internet-based matchmaking agencies. Aside from the perception others in their social environment may have of this practice, some people may also feel that admitting to this method of introduction will make their visa applications weaker.
29. This statistic is from an INS study; see Scholes 1999 and Francese 2004, who notes that "for every two marriages, there is approximately one divorce" (41). How-ever, statistics on this are difficult to verify, and other research would suggest the opposite is true for Russian-American marriages; see Trevitt 2002.
30. "A Foreign Affair," http://www.loveme.com.
31. See "A Foreign Affair" for an example of romance tour organizers.
32. Rainsford 2002.
33. Rainsford 2002; see also USCIS 1999a.

4. Valentina

1. "People with university diplomas or some university education account for 60% of the Russian immigrants to Australia; 59% to Canada; 48% to the US; and 32.5% to Israel. The number of Russian specialists in the fields of high technol-ogy and programmers is estimated at 130,000 in the US, and 50,000 in Germany." Korobkov and Zaionchkovskaia 2004: 500.
2. Rumer 2000.
3. "Despite a booming oil industry, one-quarter of the Russian population still lives

below the poverty line, and the vast majority struggle to survive on meager salaries." Orlova 2004: 20.

4. Clark and Sacks 2004: 525ff.

5. Ibid.: 541ff.

6. See Corrin 1999.

7. See Korobkov and Zaionchkovskaia (2004: 287) for a discussion of migration in the Commonwealth of Independent States.

8. Sperling 2003: 239.

9. For a discussion of the social situation and labor statistics in the republics during the late Soviet period, see Molyneux 1981; Lubin 1984; Pilkington 1992.

10. "Trafficking has an ethnic dimension. Minorities often experience difficulties in the formal labour market and may be discriminated against. In Estonia and Latvia, ethnic Russians find it difficult to find formal employment. As a result, there are large numbers of Russian women prostitutes in Riga and Tallinn" (Wennerholm 2002: 13).

11. It should be mentioned that not all of this increase is a response to the "freedom" to migrate. Korobkov and Zaionchkovskaia point out that "nationalism, territorial claims, separatism, and the hegemonic inclinations have led to the development of ethnic conflicts and the mass flows of refugees, displaced persons, and forced migrants. These processes have pushed aside the classical migration coordinators, such as urbanization, labor market, and education market. These were replaced by the desire to acquire ethnic security. Thus in the years immediately following the USSR's dissolution, forced repatriation became the dominant migration flow, as happened previously in the years immediately following the 1917 Bolshevik revolution" (2004: 492).

12. Korobkov and Zaionchkovskaia 2004: 487.

13. Ashwin and Lytkina 2004: 189–206.

14. Corrin 1992: 16.

15. This figure is based on survey studies. Official Soviet statistics from the time did not show gender differences. See Katarina Katz's work on gender and employment in the Soviet Union, in which she writes, "In 1989, 84% of textile workers were women, but 89% of industrial welders were men. In the healthcare sector 81% of employees were women, while women made up only 25% of construction workers. The female dominated sectors had the lowest salaries. Within each sector one found fewer women the further up the career hierarchy one came. 67% of doctors were women, but 98% of nurses and assistants" (1995: 33). See also Katz 1994.

16. Pilkington 1992: 185.

17. Statistics can be deceptive, but Grogan's work suggests the possibility of improvement. "The retrospective evidence provided by the ISITO survey suggests that women were more likely than men to be non-employed in both January 1993

and January 1995 and to enter non-employment from jobs begun after January 1991. Substantial differences between the sexes in other aspects of labor force behavior are apparent. Women had much lower rates of job-to-job transitions than men in both the stock and flow samples of the ISITO and were particularly unlikely to flow into self-employment. Several studies published in the early years of Russian economic transition proclaimed a 'female face of Russian unemployment,' based on the observation that there were more women than men officially registered as unemployed. However, despite the higher tendency of females to exit post-Soviet jobs to non-employment, by January 1998 it did not appear that females were more likely to be non-employed than males. . . . females had relatively short unemployment durations in the 1994–96 period, thus suggesting that the situation for women on the labor market may have improved over time" (Grogan 2003: 420). Ashwin and Lytkina (2004: 189–206) also suggest that there may be more men than women unemployed, though the large black and gray labor market makes such figures very imprecise.

18. Katz 1995: 34.
19. Orlova 2004: 15.
20. Petrova 2005.
21. Clarke 1999: 328.
22. The discrimination against women in the workplace is so glaring from a Western perspective that even the *Economist* has commented on it: "In theory, employers found guilty of sexual harassment face up to three years in prison. In practice, the law—like many laws in Russia—is rarely enforced. Some employers demand sex from female employees with impunity. The Moscow-based Fund for Protection from Sexual Harassment at Work blacklists 300 firms where women are known to have been harassed or assaulted. Its director, Valery Vikulov, says that some women in Moscow have even reported being raped at the job interview. Russia is still a man's world. When Tatyana Paramonova was made acting head of the Central Bank, several Russian newspapers seemed more interested in her views on cooking than on monetary policy. Women who call themselves feministki are greeted with ill-disguised contempt—and not only by men. Most Russians usually regard feminism as a species of western subversion, rather as many of them thought of economic reform in 1992. 'At the moment, the reaction is negative,' admits Lyudmila Zavadskaya, one of the parliamentarians from Women of Russia. 'But they will get used to it' " (12 August 1995, 44).
23. Clarke 1999.
24. *Women's International Network News (WIN NEWS)* 29(4) (2003): 75.
25. La Font 2001: 209.
26. Petrova 2005.
27. See Gaddy and Ickes 2002. For a critical discussion of the term, see Krueger and Linz 2002: 31–44.

28. Ashwin 1999.

29. "S. Clarke found that well-paying de novo enterprises preferred to recruit workers from other jobs, suggesting that workers may have preferred to have even nonpaying jobs that gave them access to this lucrative section of the labor market." Grogan 2003: 420.

30. Clarke 1999: 196ff.

5. Tanya

1. Examples can be found in Muir 2003 and Holt 2002.

2. "Trafficking of human beings . . . is now a multi-billion dollar industry run by individuals and small and large organised criminal networks. . . . experts agree that a disproportionate number of trafficked persons are women and girls." Jordan 2002: 28.

3. See, for examples, Digges 1998 and Specter 1998.

4. Jordan notes that corruption, perhaps because of economic decline, plays a role in trafficking from the former Soviet Union. "As the socialist systems and economies of the former Soviet Union and elsewhere collapsed, some civil servant salaries fell below the poverty level. As a result, criminal activities in many countries are organised by, or with the co-operation of, officials. Corruption is so extensive in some countries that victims who escape and report to the police risk being sent back to the traffickers. Under these conditions, traffickers no longer need to build walls or put bars on windows" (2002: 29).

5. Vannoy et al. 1999.

6. Johnson (2001: 153) cites the U.S. Department of State's 1997 reporting of statistics from the Russian Ministry of Internal Affairs for this figure.

7. Women's International Network News 2003: 54.

8. Johnson 2001: 153.

9. This is cited in Johnson's article; she then goes on to write, disturbingly, "When police allow that they can intervene in woman battery, they often claim that women provoke their own battery, making neither the batterer nor the police responsible for preventing the violence. Provocation includes a wide variety of behaviours, such as earning too much money, wearing the wrong clothes, being unfaithful, taunting the abuser, nagging, and complaining about bad behavior. For example, a police officer told a woman who was claiming battery, 'It is no accident he is beating you because you must be so hard to live with' " (2001: 156).

10. Ibid.: 160.

11. Babitskaya quoted in Lambroschini 2001.

12. Women's International Network News 2002a. See also Women's International Network News 2002b.

13. And women's voices are being heard less frequently in politics, too. "Political

representation, notwithstanding the success of the Women's party, is now far lower than during the communist period." Waters and Posadskaya 1995: 352.

14. In her book on women's movements in a global perspective, Basu states that "women's movements in China, Russia, and Eastern Europe tend to be more concerned with public domain questions such as employment, political representation, and social security. One possible explanation for this difference in focus concerns the varying relationship of the private to the public cross-nationally. In liberal democracies, where the public and private are sharply demarcated, women's movements have sought to reveal the 'secrets' concealed in the private realm. In communist nations with fewer barriers between the public and private spheres, feminists are suspicious of state scrutiny of the private domain" (1995: 11–12).

15. Sperling et al. 2001: 1170. International activism (feminist or otherwise) is tricky and controversial at many levels. Not only is the debate about which issues are most pertinent to address difficult to maneuver but the issue of who benefits from the activism is also charged. Sperling et al. note, for example (2001: 1176), that American feminist activists in Russia are sometimes regarded with suspicion stemming from the feeling that the Russian activists are being milked for experiences that can be used to further the American activists' careers in the West.

16. Basu 1995: 1.

17. See Enloe 1989, a seminal text.

18. One result and example of this is the way global feminist alliances are often more easily made between middle-class women across national boundaries than with women of different classes and races within a nation. Grewal and Kaplan (1994) have written a critique of the universalizing tendencies of global feminism. For a more recent discussion, see Davis (2002), in which she analyzes global feminism in practice through the different versions of *Our Bodies Our Selves* that have been published around the world.

19. Moore 2003: 95ff.

20. See the work of La Strada (http://www.lastradainternational.org), an organization which is combating trafficking in women in Eastern and Central Europe.

21. See Holt 2002. Work with prostitutes in India would suggest that this is sometimes the case there, as well; see Jana et al. 2002. Two recent books on trafficking and prostitution explore the agency of sex workers and their livelihood strategies, including the relationship of trafficking to global capitalism and transnational migration: see Kempadoo and Doezema 1998 and Kempadoo et al. 2005.

22. This situation is poignantly portrayed in the film *Show Me Love (Lilja 4-Ever)*, by Lucas Moodysson.

23. United Nations ODCCP 2000.

24. The definition continues, "Exploitation shall include, at a minimum, the exploitation of the prostitution of others or other forms of sexual exploitation (interpretative note 64), forced labour or services, slavery or practices similar to slavery,

servitude or the removal of organs." See Williams and Masika 2002 for a discussion of the background and implications of this definition's wording. Among other things, they note that "by making coercion and deception central to the definition of trafficking, it does not require governments to consider all prostitution to be trafficking, and thus illegal. What the Protocol fails to do, however, is to require signatories to extend assistance and human rights protection to trafficked persons" (4).

25. Williams and Masika 2002: 5.

26. Ibid.: 4.

27. Wennerholm 2002: 11. See also O'Neill 1999; Jordan 2002: 28.

28. Williams and Masika 2002: 6.

29. Ibid.: 8. I guess that is the kind of comment one would expect from a scary, American feminist.

30. Jordan 2002: 28.

31. Wennerholm 2002: 12.

32. Williams and Masika 2002: 5.

33. Ibid.

34. Jordan 2002: 29.

35. For a description of how this has happened in the meat-slaughtering industry and the effects it has on both employees and industry, see Schlosser 2001. For examples from the chicken industry, see Grimsley 2001.

36. Barnes et al. 2001.

37. Jana et al. approach the role of labor regulations in trafficking directly when they state: "If the entire employment market, in both formal and unorganised sectors, could be regulated in adherence to national and international labour laws protecting the rights of workers, and if all workers were conscious of their labour rights, were organised, and had a role in regulating the workplace, the demand of trafficked labour would cease to exist" (Jana et al. 2002: 70ff.). Jordan is adamant that "governments must reform their immigration laws to allow people to migrate legally to meet the domestic demand for labour" (2002: 34).

38. Dell'orto 2001.

39. Lawrence et al. 2004.

40. Robertson 2000.

41. For a discussion of a recent example, see Arie 2004.

42. "The Human Rights Caucus focuses on the rights of trafficking victims. It recognises the difference between forced and voluntary prostitution, presenting sex work as a legitimate labour option for women, one in which women have agency, and for which they should not be penalised, morally or legally. The Coalition Against Trafficking in Women (CATW), problematises prostitution in itself as an extreme form of gender discrimination, and thus as a violation of women's fundamental human rights." Williams and Masika 2002: 4.

43. Jordan 2002: 30.

44. This has been the case in Belgium and the Netherlands, and the basis for EU directives for helping victims of trafficking is the Belgium model; see Pearson 2002: 56ff. In the United States, this policy was instituted through the Victims of Trafficking and Violence Protection Act of 2000 (HR 3244). An explanation of how it is used can be found in U.S. Department of State 2004: section VI.

45. Jana et al. 2002: 73.

46. Pearson 2002: 58.

47. Holt 2002.

48. Williams and Masika 2002: 8.

49. Tzvetkova 2002: 61.

50. Those who suggest the human rights approach to the issue of trafficking claim that such an approach would shift "the focus away from seeing trafficked persons as objects towards understanding them as people bearing human rights. It also overcomes anti-immigrant bias, misogyny, and contempt towards those trafficked persons who are also voluntary sex workers. The human rights framework dictates an empowerment approach to assisting trafficked persons in retaking control over their lives and in ensuring that women are treated as adults, not children" (Jordan 2002: 30). Such an approach, which also would legitimate sex work as a conscious labor choice, would demand granting Third World women "the same degree of self-awareness, autonomy, and agency that is taken as self-evident for Western women" (Doezema 2002: 25). See also Jana et al. 2002: 78.

51. Tzvetkova 2002: 63.

52. The 1994 Violence against Women Act allows a woman to self-petition for a visa if she can show that she has been physically battered or suffered extreme mental cruelty by her spouse. For a discussion of how this is applied in practice, and the difficulties faced by immigrant women in negotiating the paperwork necessary for self-petition, see Free and Fields 2003.

53. Jordan 2002: 34.

54. One of the more well-known cases involves a young woman from Kyrgyzstan who was found murdered by her much older husband in Washington state. When his case came to trial it was discovered that the husband was already divorced from a previous foreign bride and had begun seeking a third shortly before killing his wife. See Crary 2003.

55. The International Marriage Broker Regulation Act was signed into law as an attachment to the Violence Against Women Act (HR 3402) in January 2006.

56. *Women's Policy, Inc.* July 16, 2004.

57. Leidholdt, interviewed in Bailey 2000.

58. Bailey 2000.

59. Smaadahl, Hernes, and Langberg 2002.

6. Marina

1. See Werbner 1999 and Walton-Roberts 2004. As Walton-Roberts notes, "women are undoubtedly the most vulnerable subjects in this transnational marriage process and exemplify why it is important to highlight the 'gendered geographies of power' evident in such interactions. This also highlights how transnational practices are not always celebratory demonstrations of immigrant agency, but can also act as a mode of transmission for the expansion and perpetuation (although often refashioned) of traditional gendered hierarchies" (371). Thus, the fact that migration is a transnational practice which develops networks of connections between and across geographically diverse locations does not mean that those networks address all the needs of all migrants, nor is access to them equal for everyone.

2. Laura Bailey writes about one of the men she interviewed: "He says he is considering using the agency because of his dissatisfaction with American women. According to him, women are too wrapped up in their careers and too embittered by previous relationships. And he doesn't want a wife whose career will compete with his own. It also doesn't hurt that the women in the catalogs are dressed to kill and drop-dead gorgeous. 'I wouldn't mind having a trophy wife,' he says with a smile." Bailey 2000.

3. Chance for Love Dating Network, http://chanceforlove.com. Consulted 29 March 2005.

4. Ibid.

5. Petrova 2005.

6. Ibid.

7. For a detailed explanation of anti-fraud policies, see the Anastasia website, http://www.russianbrides.com, consulted 29 March 2005.

8. Clark and Sacks give a delineation between the different types of cities that can be used in social economic research: "Russian cities fall into four categories: the first category consists of St. Petersburg and Moscow; the second category is composed of the regional capitals (for example, Yaroslavl' is the capital city of the region in which Rybinsk is located); the third category consists of mid-sized, industrial cities with relatively diverse economies; and the fourth category is made up of either smaller cities or towns, or cities located in extreme geographical locations with fairly undiversified economies. The majority of the Russian population lives in category three" (2004: 530).

9. Many women do choose to go home during this first trial period. According to the 1999 report to Congress, "Approximately 1,100 more fiancé(e)s arrived per year on average in the 1970's and 1980's than adjusted to permanent resident alien status, and in the 1990's the average yearly excess of arrivals over adjustments has been 2,200." USCIS 1999a.

10. As part of this research, I analyzed the discourse on a number of these sites and joined in a Web-based discussion group.
11. Global7network, http://www.global7network.com, consulted on 2 February 2005.
12. Ibid.
13. Ibid.
14. Ibid.
15. Studies of the textbooks used to teach English in Russia show that the content of these books has changed dramatically since the dissolution of the USSR, and the capitalist system is now presented as a good thing, with "heroes" of the American economic system like Henry Ford portrayed positively. Pauels and Fox 2004: 116.
16. Anastasia website, consulted 29 March 2005.
17. See Avseenko (2003: 208) for a discussion of this program's format and its similarities to American talk shows like the *Oprah Winfrey Show* and the *Ricki Lake Show*.
18. Global7network, consulted 2 February 2005.
19. Ibid.
20. La Font 2001: 211.
21. Global7network, consulted 2 February 2005.
22. Ibid.
23. See Visson 2001.
24. Variations of this observation appear on a number of different sites (consulted 29 March 2005).
25. Global7network, consulted 2 February 2005.
26. Petrova 2005.
27. Ibid.
28. Azhgikhina and Goscilo 1996.
29. In her study of men interested in mail-order brides from Latin America, Schaeffer-Grabiel suggests that the use of these terms is an attempt to "class up" the language of marriage (2005: 333).
30. Petrova 2005.

7. Anastasia and John

1. There are several books and e-books like this on the market. See *Russian Bride Travel Guide* published by A Foreign Affair (http://www.loveme.com); *Love Letters . . . from Russia* by Weston Rogers (Weston Productions, 1993); and *Your Russian Bride—The Shocking Truth* by Marina Smiley (http://www.truthabout russianbrides.com) for samples of the genre.
2. See Bakardjieva 2003.

3. Spivak, the owner of a Russian-American matchmaking agency based in the United States, as quoted in Bailey 2000.

4. See A Foreign Affair.

5. For a detailed description of this process, see Trevitt 2002.

6. Petrova 2005.

7. Actually, according to the USCIS, immigrants who have applied for a green card can travel abroad as long as they petition for and receive an "advance parole" which grants permission to reenter the country, but this is another set of forms to fill in, the processing time for the application can also be drawn out, permission can be denied, and application alone costs $165, excluding fees for any biometric tests that may need to be done (see http://uscis.gov).

8. Parrenas's work (2001) on Filipina domestic workers in the United States and Italy makes this point as she traces how educated, middle-class women from the Philippines become domestic servants in their new countries.

9. The United States stills falls far behind the Scandinavian countries, however, in both the sharing of household tasks between men and women and gender empowerment for women. See Batalova and Cohen 2002.

10. For an analysis of the global and local power dynamics of American weddings, see Ingraham 1999.

8. A Catalogue of Hope

1. Another migration option for younger women is to enter the European Union or the United States on a student visa, but this generally requires a significant amount of capital.

2. This sounds like a lot, but it is still only 3 or 4 percent of the brides who immigrate to the United States each year, and only 0.4 percent of the total number of immigrants. Most of these mail-order brides come from the CIS and the Philippines (USCIS 1999b).

3. Constable, in her work on Southeast Asian mail-order brides, proposes the notion of transnationalism and transnational marriage. She writes, "In contrast to notions of migration and trafficking, which are viewed as geographically one-directional and one-dimensional in terms of power, the recent literature on transnationalism considers multidirectional flows of desires, people, ideas, and objects across, between, and beyond national boundaries" (2003: 215ff.).

4. This is how Vertovec (2004: 1–2) defines the term, but as Grewal and Kaplan point out, the term "transnationalism" is used to mean different things in the academy. It is being used to describe migration, the demise of the nation-state, as a synonym for "diasporic," in conjunction with global movements of financial capital and corporations, and as a way of describing international NGOs and activism (2001: 664–66).

5. Walton-Roberts 2004: 362.

6. Hirsch 2003; Vertovec 2004: 9; Walton-Roberts 2004: 367.

7. See http://www.russianbrides.com/ads.html and http://www.loveme.com/personals.

8. See Schaeffer-Grabiel, who notes that "women from Colombia, Asia, Russia and Japan similarly justify their search for foreign men by degrading local men, which reveals how far-reaching this 'personal' gender revolution has spread" (2004: 40).

9. This explanation was suggested by Schaeffer-Grabiel, who has researched Mexican mail-order brides. "By defining Mexican men as macho, women degrade the Mexican nation to construct themselves as having a more cosmopolitan affinity with the U.S. nation" (2004: 33).

10. Luehrmann discusses the way people who know Russian women writing to foreign men are also implicated in this discourse. "By implying that Russian women have to turn to foreign men because real Russian men have become a rarity, they relieved young women of the charge of betraying the nation but also made light of the problems these women faced, be it in trying to lead tolerable lives in Russia or in leaving their country on the invitation of men they hardly know. Like the media discourse on Russian gender imbalance and demographic decline, conversations such as these simultaneously reinforce the idea that it is a woman's foremost aim to find a husband and that it is very difficult to do so in Russia. Another sub-text of this conversation is the opinion, expressed by scholars as well as by many of my female interlocutors, that men have been harder hit than women by the changes of post-Soviet life, because male identities were tied more strongly to their status of worker in the Soviet economy" (2004: 868).

11. One striking quote in particular stands out as being stuck on the idea that American women are unattractive on the international market. "While there is little demand among foreign men for American wives, there is a huge demand for American husbands. Thousands of foreign women are seeking husbands in the international bride market." See Scholes 1997.

12. The 1999 report to Congress (USCIS 1999a) took up these different views: "Polarized views exist of the relationships and marriages that result from the use of IMOs [international matchmaking organizations]. At one end of the spectrum is the view that the mail-order bride business is an international personal ad service used by 'consenting adults [and] competent people.' [. . .] The other end of the spectrum challenges the inequities of these transactions and identifies the mail-order bride phenomenon as an international industry that often trafficks women from developing countries to industrialized Western countries."

13. See, for example, Butler 1990.

14. Scholes (1997: under "The Reasons for Mail-Order Marriages") notes that "many Taiwanese men prefer brides from other Asian countries because they feel Taiwanese women—who tend to be better educated and more affluent—expect

too much from their husbands. Due to this attitude, Taiwan has imposed a limit on the number of brides from certain countries that can enter Taiwan each year . . . On the women's side, many of them are seeking Western men since, they say, Taiwanese men want to marry only hard-working, obedient drudges while Taiwanese women have discarded this traditional role and are seeking equality and mutual respect in marriage."

15. Kojima 2001.

16. See Schaeffer-Grabiel 2005: 338. Schaeffer-Grabiel also discusses how, in discourse about these relationships, America is constructed as a biologically masculine nation and Latin America (one of the sites of her research) as a feminine location as a way of naturalizing the relationships that develop through mail-order bride searches (343).

17. A parallel can be drawn to the argument Grewal and Kaplan put forward when they discuss the way sexualities are produced in the current globalized context: "Nation-states, economic formations, consumer cultures, and forms of governmentality all work together to produce and uphold subjectivities and communities" (2001: 670).

18. This is addressed by the term "intersectionalilty." For analysis of these factors and details of the way class, race, sexuality, and nationality are constructed across and by borders, see Grimes 1998 and Hirsch 2003 on Mexican migrants.

19. Strong, capable, unsubmissive Russian women appear in literature (see, e.g., the novel by Gladkov, *Cement*, discussed in chapter 2), in Soviet-era research on Russian culture (see Gray 1989), in historical work on women in the Soviet bloc and their political importance (Penn 2005), and in comments in the discussion groups from men who have married Russian women.

20. In her recent article about the masculinities displayed by men who are looking for Latin American mail-order brides, Schaeffer-Grabiel notes that "scholarship on the mail-order bride industry in Asia and Russia tends to emphasize the exploitation of poor women in developing countries by Western men as part of the sexual trafficking trade, an emphasis that reproduces binary relations of power between developing and first-world countries" (2005: 331).

21. Another example of how important marriage is for Russian women, even if it ends in divorce, can be seen in the stories of the women who were forced into labor camps and exiled as political prisoners during the mass arrests of the 1930s. Most of these women were arrested not because of political mistakes they may or may not have made themselves but because they were married to or the daughters of middle-ranking bureaucrats in the Soviet regime. The state created a personal identity for the women based on their connections to the men in their lives and then went on to prosecute them for this connection. See Clements 2003: 161–64.

22. Kay 2000: 267.

23. Letherby and Marchband 2003; see also Jones 1997 and Hughes 1999.
24. Amnesty International and other groups have supported the International Marriage Broker Regulation Act (IMBRA), which Bush signed into law in January 2006.
25. Bakardjieva 2003: 308; see also Hardey 2004.

Bibliography

Arie, Sofie. 2004. "A Storm in a Port." *Guardian*, 13 July 2004.

Ashwin, Sarah. 1999. *Russian Workers: The Anatomy of Patience*. Manchester: Manchester University Press.

Ashwin, Sarah, and Tatyana Lytkina. 2004. "Men in Crisis in Russia: The Role of Domestic Marginalization." *Gender and Society* 18(2): 189–206.

Avseenko, Natalya. 2003. "American Programs and Their Effectiveness on Russian Television." *American Studies International* 41(1–2): 203–19.

Azhgikhina, Nadezhda. 1995. "Myt, mutant, miss." *Bang* no. 3:10–13.

Azhgikhina, Nadezhda, and Helena Goscilo. 1996. "Getting under Their Skin: The Beauty Salon in Russian Women's Lives." In Helena Goscilo and Beth Holmgren, eds., *Russia, Women, Culture*. Bloomington: Indiana University Press.

Bailey, Laura. 2000. "From Russia, with Love." PopPolitics.com, 19 June.

Bakardjieva, Maria. 2003. "Virtual Togetherness: An Everyday-Life Perspective." *Media, Culture and Society* 25(3): 291–313.

Baldwin, Kate. 2002. *Beyond the Color Line and the Iron Curtain: Reading Encounters between Black and Red, 1922–1963*. Durham, N.C.: Duke University Press.

Barnes, Edward, Paul Cuadros, David Hendee, and Elaine Shannon. 2001. "Illegal but Fighting for Rights." *Time*, 15 January.

Basu, Amrita. 1995. *The Challenge of Local Feminisms: Women's Movements in Global Perspective*. Boulder, Colo.: Westview Press.

Batalova, Jeanne, and Philip Cohen. 2002. "Premarital Cohabitation and Housework: Couples in Cross-National Perspective." *Journal of Marriage and Family* 64 (August): 743–55.

Bock von Wülfingen, Betina. 2005. "Geschlechtskörper—Hormonell Stabilisiert oder Flexibilisiert? Das Lesbenhormon." In Corinna Bath, Bettina Bock von Wülfingen, Angelika Saupe, and Jutta Weber, eds., *Materialität Denken—Studien zur Technologischen Verkörperung* (Thinking Materiality—Studies on Technological Embodiments). Bielefeld: Transkript Verlag.

Brook, Heather. 2002. "Stalemate: Rethinking the Politics of Marriage." *Feminist Theory* 3(1): 45–66.

Butler, Judith. 1990. *Gender Trouble: Feminism and the Subversion of Identity*. New York: Routledge.

Clark, Carol, and Michael Sacks. 2004. "A View from Below: Industrial Re-Structuring and Women's Employment at Four Russian Enterprises." *Communist and Post-Communist Studies* 37 (2004): 523–45.

Clarke, Simon. 1999. *The Formation of a Labour Market in Russia*. Northampton, Mass.: Edward Elgar.

Clements, Barbara. 2003. Review of *Remembering the Darkness: Women in Soviet Prisons*, ed. and trans. Veronica Shapovaloc, and *Till My Tale Is Told: Women's Memoirs of the Gulag*, ed. Simeon Vilensky. *National Women's Studies Association Journal* 15(2): 161–64.

Clements, Barbara, Rebecca Friedman, and Dan Healey, eds. 2002. *Russian Masculinities: History and Culture*. New York: Palgrave.

Constable, Nicole. 2003. *Romance on a Global Stage: Pen Pals, Virtual Ethnography, and "Mail-Order" Marriages*. Berkeley: University of California Press.

Corrin, Chris, ed. 1992. *Superwoman and the Double Burden: Women's Experiences of Change in Central and Eastern Europe and the Former Soviet Union*. London: Scarlet Press.

Corrin, Chris. 1999. *Gender and Identity in Central and Eastern Europe*. London: Frank Cass.

Coupland, Justine. 1996. "Dating Advertisements: Discourses of the Commodified Self." *Discourse and Society* 7(2): 187–207.

Crary, David. 2003. "Bill May Protect Mail-Order Brides." *Holland Sentinel National Online*, 6 July.

Cubbins, Lisa, and Dana Vannoy. 2004. "Division of Household Labor as a Source of Contention for Married and Cohabiting Couples in Metropolitan Moscow." *Journal of Family Issues* 25(2): 182–215.

Davis, Kathy. 2002. "Feminist Body/Politics as World Traveller: Translating *Our Bodies, Ourselves*." *European Journal of Women's Studies* 9(3): 223–47.

Dell'orto, Giovanna. 2001. "14 Mexicans Die in Border Crossing." *Washington Post*, 24 May.

Digges, Charles. 1998. "Recruiters Fool Women into Prostitution." *St. Petersburg Times*, 23–29 March.

Doezema, Jo. 2002. "Who Gets to Choose? Coercion, Consent, and the UN Trafficking Protocol." *Gender and Development* 10(1): 20–27.

Ekéus, Carolina. 1995. "Skitliv ger skitsex." *Bang* no. 3: 16–20.

Enloe, Cynthia. 1989. *Bananas, Beaches and Bases: Making Feminist Sense of International Politics*. Berkeley: University of California Press.

Fleming, P., A. Meyroyan, and I. Klimova. 1994. "Alcohol Treatment Services in Russia: A Worsening Crisis." *Alcohol and Alcoholism* 29(4): 357–62.

Fodor, Eva. 2002. "Gender and the Experience of Poverty in Eastern Europe and Russia after 1989." *Communist and Post-Communist Studies* 35: 369–82.

Francese, Peter. 2004. "Marriage Drain's Big Cost." *American Demographics* 26(3): 40–41.

Free, Bob, and Penny Fields. 2003. "Representing the Most Vulnerable." *Bar News.* Washington State Bar Association. December. www.wsba.org.

Gaddy, Clifford, and Barry Ickes. 2002. *Russia's Virtual Economy*. Washington, D.C.: Brookings Institution Press.

Gemzöe, Lena. 1995. "Kvinnoforskning med förhinder." *Bang*, no. 3: 36–37.

Gladkov, Fedor. 1994. [1924]. *Cement*. Chicago: Northwestern Publishing House.

Gray, Francine du Plessix. 1989. *Soviet Women: Walking the Tightrope*. London: Doubleday.

Grewal, Inderpal, and Caren Kaplan. 1994. *Scattered Hegemonies: Postmodernity and Transnational Feminist Practices*. Minneapolis: University of Minnesota Press.

———. 2001. "Global Identities: Theorizing Transnational Studies of Sexuality." *GLQ* 7(4): 663–79.

Grimes, Kimberly. 2003. [1998]. *Crossing Borders: Changing Social Identities in Southern Mexico*. Tucson: University of Arizona Press.

Grimsley, Kirstin Downey. 2001. "Tyson Foods Indicted in INS Probe: U.S. Says Firm Sought Illegal Immigrants." *Washington Post*, 20 December.

Grogan, Louise. 2003. "Worker Flows in the Russian Economic Transition: Longitudinal Evidence from Four Cities." *Economic Development and Cultural Change* 51(2): 399–425.

Hardey, John. 2004. "Mediated Relationships: Authenticity and the Possibility of Romance." *Information, Communication and Society* 7(2): 207–22.

Hesford, Victoria. 2005. "Feminism and its Ghosts: The Spectre of the Feminist-as-Lesbian." *Feminist Theory* 6(3): 227–50.

Hirsch, Francine. 2002. "Race without the Practice of Racial Politics." *Slavic Review* 61(1): 30–43.

Hirsch, Jennifer. 2003. *A Courtship after Marriage: Sexuality and Love in Mexican Transnational Families*. Berkeley: University of California Press.

Holt, Kate. 2002. "Once They Were Girls: Now They Are Slaves." *Observer*, 3 February.

Hughes, Donna. 1999. "The Internet and the Global Prostitution Industry." In S. Hawthorne and R. Klein, eds., *CyberFeminism: Connectivity, Critique and Creativity*. North Melbourne: Spinifex Press.

Ingraham, Chrys. 1999. *White Weddings: Romancing Heterosexuality in Popular Culture*. New York: Routledge.

Jagger, Elizabeth. 2005. "Is Thirty the New Sixty? Dating, Age and Gender in a Postmodern, Consumer Society." *Sociology* 39(1): 89–106.

Jana, Smarajit, Nandinee Bandyopadhyay, Mrinal Kanti Dutta, and Amitrajit Saha. 2002. "A Tale of Two Cities: Shifting the Paradigm of Anti-Trafficking Programmes." *Gender and Development* 10(1): 69–79.

Johnson, Janet. 2001. "Privatizing Pain: The Problem of Woman Battery in Russia." *National Women's Studies Association Journal* 13(3): 153–68.

Jones, Steven G., ed. 1997. *Virtual Culture: Identity and Communication in Cybersociety*. London: Sage Publications.

Jordan, Ann D. 2002. "Human Rights or Wrongs? The Struggle for a Rights-Based Response to Trafficking in Human Beings." *Gender and Development* 10(1): 28–37.

Jürna, Irina. 1995. Interview. *Bang* no. 3: 15.

Katz, Katarina. 1994. "Gender Differentiation and Discrimination: A Study of Soviet Wages." Ph.D. diss., Göteborg University.

———. 1995. "Lika lön." *Bang* no. 3: 32–35.

Kay, Rebecca. 2000. *Russian Women and Their Organizations: Gender, Discrimination, and Grassroots Women's Organizations, 1991–96*. New York: St. Martin's Press.

Kempadoo, Kamala, and Jo Doesema, eds. 1998. *Global Sex Workers: Rights, Resistance, and Redefinition*. New York: Routledge.

Kempadoo, Kamala, et al. 2005. *Trafficking and Prostitution Reconsidered: New Perspectives on Migration, Sex, Work, and Human Rights*. Boulder: Paradigm.

Kojima, Yu. 2001. "In the Business of Cultural Reproduction: Theoretical Implications of the Mail-Order Bride Phenomenon." *Women's Studies International Forum* 24(2): 199–210.

Korobkov, Andrei, and Zhanna Zaionchkovskaia. 2004. "The Changes in the Migration Patterns in the Post-Soviet States: The First Decade." *Communist and Post-Communist Studies* 37: 481–508.

Kotiranta, Matti, ed. 2000. *Religious Transition in Russia*. Helsinki: Kikimora.

Krueger, Gary, and Susan Linz. 2002. "Virtual Reality: Barter and Restructuring in Russian Industry." *Problems of Post-Communism* 49(5): 31–44.

Kuhn, Randall, and Steven Stillman. 2004. "Understanding Interhousehold Transfers in a Transition Economy: Evidence from Russia." *Economic Development and Cultural Change* 53(1): 131–56.

La Font, Suzanne. 2001. "One Step Forward, Two Steps Back: Women in the Post-Communist States." *Communist and Post-Communist Studies* 34: 203–20.

Lambroschini, Sophie. 2001. "Russia: Domestic Violence Persists." Radio Free Europe/ Radio Liberty, 7 March. www.rferl.org.

Lawrence, Felicity, Hsiao-Hung Pai, Vikram Dodd, Helen Carter, David Ward, and Jonathan Watts. 2004. "Victims of the Sands and the Snakeheads: 19 Chinese Drown Half a World Away from Home: The Gangs behind the Tragedy Are on the Run." *Guardian*, 7 February.

Letherby, Gyle, and Jen Marchband. 2003. "Cyber-Chattels: Buying Brides and Babies on the Net." In Yvonne Jewkes, ed., *Dot.cons: Crime, Deviance, and Identity on the Internet*. Cullumpton: Willan Press.

Lubin, Nancy. 1984. *Labour and Nationality in Soviet Central Asia: An Uneasy Compromise*. Princeton: Princeton University Press.

Luehrmann, Sonja. 2004. "Mediated Marriage: Internet Matchmaking in Provincial Russia." *Europe-Asia Studies* 56(6): 857–75.

Molyneux, Francine. 1981. "Women in Socialist Societies: Problems of Theory and Practice." In Young et al., eds., *Of Marriage and the Market*. London: CSE Books.

Moore, Elizabeth. 2003. "The Twain Shall Meet: American Studies in Post-Soviet Russia." *American Studies International* 41(1–2): 82–99.

Muir, Hugh. 2003. "Ruthless Human Trafficker Jailed for 10 Years." *Guardian*, 23 December.

Olcott, Martha Brill. 1995. "Central Asia: The Calculus of Independence." *Current History* 94(594): 337–42.

Orlova, Alexandra. 2004. "From Social Dislocation to Human Trafficking: The Russian Case." *Problems of Post-Communism* 51(6): 14–22.

Osborn, Andrew. 2004. "Russia Fails to Ban Drinking in Public despite Soaring Alcoholism." *British Medical Journal* 329: 1202.

Parrenas, Rhacel Salazar. 2001. *Servants of Globalization: Women, Migration, and Domestic Work*. Stanford, Calif.: Stanford University Press.

Pauels, Wolfgang, and Thomas Fox. 2004. "The Representation of the USA in EFL Textbooks in the Soviet Union and Russia." *America Studies International* 42(1): 92–122.

Pearson, Elaine. 2002. "Half-Hearted Protection: What Does Victim Protection Really Mean for Victims of Trafficking in Europe?" *Gender and Development* 10(1): 56–59.

Penn, Shana. 2005. *Solidarity's Secret: The Women Who Defeated Communism in Poland*. Ann Arbor: University of Michigan Press.

Peterson, Dale. 2002. *Up from Bondage: The Literature of Russian and American Soul*. Durham, N.C.: Duke University Press.

Petrova, Elena. 2005. *Russian Brides Cyber Guide: A Russian Woman about Russian Women*. http://www.womenrussia.com.

Pilkington, Hilary. 1992. "Russia and the Former Soviet Republics." In Chris Corrin, ed., *Superwoman and the Double Burden: Women's Experiences of Change in Central and Eastern Europe and the Former Soviet Union*. London: Scarlet Press.

Pleck, Elizabeth. 2003. *Cinderella Dreams: The Allure of the Lavish Wedding*. Berkeley: University of California Press.

Rainsford, Sarah. 2002. " 'Romance Tourists' Head East." *BBC News: Europe*, 9 July.

Reed, Kate. 2004. "The Eclipse of Marriage. Bringing Debates Back into Sociological Accounts of Health." *European Journal of Women's Studies* 11(1): 61–76.

Robertson, Nic. 2000. "Britain, EU Launch Major Investigation after Deaths of Smuggled Immigrants." *CNN.com*, 19 June.

Rotkirch, Anna. 2000. *The Man Question: Loves and Lives in Late Twentieth Century Russia*. Helsinki: University of Helsinki Press.

Rumer, Boris, ed. 2000. *Central Asia and the New Global Economy*. Armonk, N.Y.: M. E. Sharpe.

Schaeffer-Grabiel, Felicity. 2004. "Cyberbrides and Global Imaginaries: Mexican Women's Turn from the National to the Foreign." *Space and Culture* 7(1): 33–48.

——. 2005. "Planet-Love.com: Cyberbrides in the Americas and the Transnational Routes of U.S. Masculinity." *Signs* 31(2): 331–56.

Schlosser, Eric. 2001. *Fast Food Nation: The Dark Side of the All-American Meal*. Boston: Houghton Mifflin.

Scholes, Robert. J. 1997. "How Many Mail-Order Brides?" *Immigration Review*, no. 28 (Spring 1997). Online. http://www.cis.org/articles/1997/IR28.

——. 1999. Appendix A to USCIS International Matchmaking Organizations: A Report to Congress News Release. U.S. Citizenship and Immigration Services.

Smaadahl, Tove, Helene Hernes, and Liv Langberg. 2002. *Drømmen om det gode liv: En rapport om utenlandske kvinner, gift med Norske menn, som måtte søke tilflukt på krisesentrene i 2001*. Oslo: Krisesentersekretariatet og Tanaprosjektet.

Specter, Michael. 1998. "Traffickers' New Cargo: Naive Slavic Women." *New York Times International*, 11 January, 1.

Sperling, Valerie. 2003. "The Last Refuge of a Scoundrel: Patriotism, Militarism and the Russian National Idea." *Nations and Nationalism* 9(2): 235–53.

Sperling, Valerie, Myra Marx Ferree, and Barbara Risman. 2001. "Constructing Global Feminism: Transnational Advocacy Networks and Russian Women's Activism." *Signs* 26(4): 1155–86.

Sun, Lena H. 1998. "The Search for Miss Right Takes a Turn toward Russia: 'Mail-Order Brides' of the '90s Are Met Via Internet and on 'Romance Tours.'" *Washington Post*, 8 March, A01.

Sweetman, Caroline. 2003. Editorial. *Gender and Development* 11(2): 2–8.

Trevitt, Jamie. 2002. "Can't Buy Me Love: A Closer Look at the Russian Mail-Order Bride Industry." Senior thesis, Duke University.

Turkle, Sherry. 1995. *Life on the Screen: Identity in the Age of the Internet*. New York: Simon and Schuster.

Tzvetkova, Marina. 2002. "NGO Responses to Trafficking in Women." *Gender and Development* 10(1): 60–68.

United Nations. Office of Drug Control and Crime Prevention (ODCCP). 2000. Trafficking protocol.

U.S. Citizenship and Immigration Services (USCIS). 1999a. *International Matchmaking Organizations: A Report to Congress*. February. http://uscis.gov.

——. 1999b. *News Release: INS Reports to Congress on Mail-Order Bride Business*. 4 March.

U.S. Department of State. 2004. *Trafficking in Persons Report 2004*. 14 June.

Vannoy, Dana, Natalia Rimashevskaya, Lisa Cubbins, Marina Malysheva, Elena Meshterkina, and Marina Pisklakova. 1999. *Marriages in Russia: Couples during the Economic Transition*. Westport, Conn.: Praeger.

Vertovec, Steven. 2004. *Trends and Impacts of Migrant Transnationalism*. Centre on Migration, Policy and Society Working Paper no. 3. Oxford: Centre on Migration, Politics and Society.

Veselá, Pavla. 2003. "The Hardening of Cement: Russian Women and Modernization." *National Women's Studies Association Journal* 15(3): 104–23.

Visson, Lynn. 2001. *Wedded Strangers: The Challenges of Russian-American Marriages*. New York: Hippocrene Books.

Walton-Roberts, Margaret. 2004. "Transnational Migration Theory in Population Geography: Gendered Practices in Networks Linking Canada and India." *Population, Space and Place* 10: 361–73.

Waters, Elizabeth, and Anastasia Posadskaya. 1995. "Democracy without Women Is No Democracy: Women's Struggles in Postcommunist Russia." In Basu, ed., *The Challenge of Local Feminisms*. Boulder, Colo.: Westview Press.

Weiner, Amir. 2002. "Nothing but Certainty." *Slavic Review* 61(1): 44–53.

Wennerholm, Carolina Johansson. 2002. "Crossing Borders and Building Bridges: The Baltic Region Networking Project." *Gender and Development* March 10(1): 10–19.

Werbner, Pnina. 1999. "Global Pathways: Working-Class Cosmopolitans and the Creation of Transnational Ethnic Worlds." *Social Anthropology* 7(1): 17–35.

Williams, Suzanne, and Rachel Masika. 2002. Editorial. *Gender and Development* 10(1): 2–9.

Women's International Network News. 2002a. "U.S. Leads World in Female Homicides." *WIN NEWS* 28(3): 65.

——. 2002b. "USA: Epidemic of Domestic Violence and Wife Assault." *WIN NEWS* 28(4): 49.

——. 2003. "Russia: Violence against Women Rampant, Condoned by Authorities." *WIN NEWS* 29(2): 54.

Women's Policy, Inc. 2004. "Senate Panel Hears Testimony on Human Trafficking and Mail Order Brides." *Women's Policy, Inc.* 10(23).

Wyatt, Caroline. 2001. "Russian Ex-Wives Fight Back." *BBC News: Europe*, 9 August.

——. 2002. "Russia Launches Population Census." *BBC News: Europe*, 15 June.

Young, Kate, Carol Wolkowits, and Roslyn McCullagh, eds. 1981. *Of Marriage and the Market: Women's Subordination Internationally and its Lessons*. London: CSE Books.

Websites

AnastasiaWeb. http://www.russianbrides.com.

Chance for Love Dating Network. http://www.chanceforlove.com.

Coalition Against Trafficking in Women. http://www.catwinternational.org.

A Foreign Affair. http://www.loveme.com.

Geneva Foundation for Medical Education and Research. http://www.gfmer.ch.

Global7network. http://www.global7network.com.

International Human Rights Law Group. http://www.hrlawgroup.org.
La Strada. http://www.lastradainternational.org.
Radio Free Europe/Radio Liberty. http://www.rferl.org.
Russian Brides. http://www.russianbrides.com/ads.html.
Russian Brides Club. http://www.russian-brides-club.com.
Russian Women. http://www.forrussianwomen.com.
Special Lady. http://www.special-lady.com.
U.S. Citizenship and Immigration Services (USCIS). http://uscis.gov.
U.S. Department of State. http://usinfo.state.gov.
Washington State Bar Association. http://www.wsba.org.
WomenRussia. http://www.womenrussia.com.
Your Russian Bride—The Shocking Truth. http://www.truthaboutrussianbrides.com.

Index

Ethnic diversity, in former Soviet Union, 42, 167 n.43, 167 n.46
Extended family, 107–108, 111–112, 116, 122, 139–140

Feminine ideal: identity and, 18, 157, 159, 180 n.21; marriage and, 180 n.21; motherhood and, 37; role in the home, 166 n.22
Feminism: American women and, 26–27, 47, 93; emancipation of Soviet women and, 30, 165 n.18, 166 n.19; global, 32, 95–96, 173 n.14, 173 n.15, 173 n.18; lesbianism and, 37–38, 167 n.37; *Mannsweiber*, 37; terminology, 36–38, 96; understanding of in Russia, 29–30, 165 nn.9–10, 166 n.35
Fiancée visa, 113, 132–133, 176 n.9; interview, 133–135, 159
Fraud, 110

Gender, enacting, 155
Gender discrimination: horizontal structure of job sectors, 72, 170 n.15; state-sanctioned, 73; in workplace, 70–73, 171 n.22
Gold diggers, 109–110, 135, 144
Green card, 113, 136–137, 178 n.7

Homesickness, 117. *See also* Culture shock

Immigrant identity, 124–127, 144, 169 n.1
INS (Immigration and Naturalization Service), 96. *See also* USCIS
International economy of desire, 155
Internationalism, 41; and national identity, 167 n.43
International Marriage Broker Regulation Act, 105, 159, 175 n.55, 181 n.24

Internet dating services, 12–13, 164 nn.3–4, 164 nn.6–7
Internet technology: access, 6, 17; usage, 17
Intersectionality, 155, 180 n.18
Isolation, 108, 120, 122, 158. *See also* Extended family

K-1 visa. *See* Fiancée visa
Kollontai, Aleksandra, 29

Mail-order brides (non-Russian nationalities), 155, 168 n.2, 179 nn.8–9, 179 n.14, 180 n.16, 180 n.20
Mail-order brides (Russian): age, 60; application process, 50–52; catalogues, printed, 8, 51; as category, 3–4, 163 n.1; commodification and objectification, 9–10; cost, 134; databases, 10; diversity, 18–19; education levels, 69; industry, 9, 49, 152, 154; Internet sites, 9–12; numbers, 178 n.2; opinions of in Russia, 39; photography and, 51–52, 78; reasons for participation, 39, 52–53, 162, 168 n.3; scams, 83–86, 109; stereotypes, 18–19, 79, 91, 93, 109, 125, 129, 176 n.2, 180 n.19; success rate, 169 nn.28–29; terminology, 124, 177 n.29; trafficking and, 12, 102–105, 179 n.12; as trope, 4; whiteness and, 18, 168 n.49, 168 n.50
Mail-order husbands: age, 61; catalogue, 61–63, 153; cost, 153; expectations of, 19–20, 82, 86–87; geographical location, 20, 44–45, 50; letter-writing techniques, 25–26, 81, 90, 131; perceived desires, 16–17, 61–63; reasons to find, 157; understanding of, 60, 91
Market instability, 74

Ericka Johnson is a research fellow at the Department of Technology and Social Change, Linköping University, in Sweden.

Library of Congress Cataloging-in-Publication Data

Johnson, Ericka
Dreaming of a mail-order husband: Russian-American internet romance /
Ericka Johnson.
p. cm.
Includes bibliographical references and index.
ISBN 978-0-8223-4010-2 (cloth : alk. paper)
ISBN 978-0-8223-4029-4 (pbk. : alk. paper)
1. Women—Russia (Federation)—Soviet conditions.
2. Mail order brides—United States—Interviews.
3. Feminism—Russia (Federation). 4. Intercountry marriage—United States.
5. Internet and women I. Title.
HQ1665.15.J64 2007
306.82—dc22   2007000705

Dreaming of a Mail-Order Husband